Strategies for University Management

Strategies for University Management

Edited by
J. Mark Munoz and Neal King

BUSINESS EXPERT PRESS

Strategies for University Management

Copyright © Business Expert Press, LLC, 2016

First published in 2016 by
Business Expert Press, LLC
222 East 46th Street, New York, NY 10017
www.businessexpertpress.com

ISBN-13: 978-1-63157-226-5 (paperback)
ISBN-13: 978-1-63157-227-2 (e-book)

Business Expert Press Strategic Management Collection

Collection ISSN: 2150-9611 (print)
Collection ISSN: 2150-9646 (electronic)

Cover and interior design by S4Carlisle Publishing Services
Private Ltd., Chennai, India

First edition: 2016

10 9 8 7 6 5 4 3 2 1

Printed in the United States of America.

Abstract

The state of affairs of contemporary higher education has been described as chaotic, highly competitive, and constrained with institutional roadblocks and bureaucracy. Despite obstacles, several academic leaders defied conventional wisdom and took on an aggressive path toward innovation and change. This book captures the viewpoints of thought leaders in the contemporary education landscape. With insights from academic administrators and experts from around the world, this book is poised to be the official "how to guide" for success in the management of educational institutions. This first volume in the series focuses on the planning and leading management functions of universities.

Keywords

University Management, University Leadership, Strategic Management, Education Management, Higher Education

Contents

CHAPTER 1

Introduction

J. Mark Munoz and Neal King

Introduction

In recent years, academic institutions worldwide have been confronted with unprecedented challenges. Survival issues have become the centerpiece of discussions in faculty meetings and boardrooms. In what have been previously depicted as "ivory towers," down-to-earth questions have emerged: How can we be profitable? How can we grow enrollment? How can we better raise funds? How can we remain relevant?

Evidence of these new challenges includes increasing number of universities whose bond ratings were downgraded, increase in the number of private 4-year colleges that were closed or acquired, incidence of mergers, aggressive tuition cuts, selling of real estate, changing educational models, and having smaller faculty (McDonald, 2014). Many academic institutions face the challenge of sustainability (Denneen & Dretler, 2012).

The corporate world has experienced rapid changes in the past 20 years. These changes have been brought about by the advent of new technologies, globalization, economic crisis, intense competition, and evolving market sophistication to name a few. With the changing operational landscape, companies needed to think in new ways and do business in nontraditional ways. The corporation 20 years ago is very different from the corporation today. In fact, even within a 5-year window, corporations can be very different. The same is true for the academic world though acceptance of this fact and adaptation have been slow to nonexistent.

Although rapid changes have been taking place in the corporate realm, a much slower pace of change has been taking place in academia. There are several reasons for this unresponsiveness: (1) History—many institutions remain grounded to their history and traditions; (2) Structure—the academic structure is one where key decisions are informed or made by committees or even the entire faculty; (3) Governance—there are matters of legality and oversight to consider; (4) Customer abundance—there is a large pool of students who are eager to earn a college degree to get a job; (5) Endowment—there are donors who are willing to share their wealth and offer financial gifts; (6) Accreditation—decisions have to be weighed in the context of its impact on institutional accreditation; (7) Lack of urgency—there are enrolled students in the pipeline and income stream is present; (8) Safety net—given the value academic institutions provide in the society and the numerous stakeholders involved, failure is oftentimes not an option. (9) A fundamental shift in the social contract, where the financial burden at all levels of post-secondary education has been transferred from the taxpayer to the individual and the family, which simultaneously narrows access based on means and often sends graduates into the work world with punishing debt.

The slow response is certainly understandable. However, what happens when: Enrollment is extremely low and budgets can't be met? Financial gifts stop coming? Online institutions intensify the competitive landscape? How can institutions cope? We see already a stark contrast between the elite privates and the resource-squeezed publics as state governments across the United States continue to de-fund higher education. Internationally, though the specifics vary from country to country, resources necessary to support meaningful and quality higher education for the citizenry as a whole are topic and priority number one.

Numerous academic institutions worldwide are facing these issues and are struggling to survive. What should be the best path to survival or better yet to achieve success?

The authors grappled with these issues for several years. It soon became evident that there is a need for a "survive and thrive guide" or handbook for academic leaders to gain new perspectives on university management for the 21st century and beyond.

This quest for finding solutions to challenges in academic administration led the editors to a global journey to find the answers. The intent was to identify innovative thinking and the best practices in university management. Insights from university leaders and experts from all over the world were gathered and included in this book.

Need for New Models

A key premise in this book is that change in academic institutions is both inevitable and urgent. A paradigm shift is necessary given the need for operational efficiency and economies of scale in order to minimize cost and increase output (Lomas, 2002; English et al., 2005; Rytmeister, 2009; Arambewela, 2010).

Academic institutions need to understand and meet stakeholder expectations, reach the right market to grow enrollment, decentralize structure, coordinate efficiently, and clarify modes of control (Willson et al., 2010). Today's undergraduates—and even more so tomorrow's—are "digital natives" who are hard-wired global citizens of a borderless virtual society of rapid change and unfettered access to contemporaries around the world. For the most part, the global professoriate does not neither understand them nor "speak their language"—yet it falls to them to prepare these young people for a whole new kind of society.

As in any industry, numerous changes take place—technology improves, consumer values shift, competition intensifies, market conditions fluctuate, globalization accelerates, and laws and policies are modified. These changes require a timely and effective response from educational institutions.

In response to change, new academic mindsets and business models are essential. These business models need to be anchored on five attributes: (1) Flexibility—to adapt and reinvent; (2) Speed—to be nimble to respond to crisis and capture opportunities in time; (3) Resourcefulness—to create exciting new value from limited resources; (4) Innovativeness—to continually find ways to improve; and (5) Connectedness—to build synergy with all its stakeholders.

In this book, the authors took the liberty of identifying a diverse set of strategic management options that are relevant to academic institutions. Specifically, attention is given to the management areas of Planning and Leading. During challenging times, the ability to plan and lead is critical. The editors are confident that the set of strategies can individually or collectively inform diverse readers and pave the way for institutional enhancement and transformation.

Importance of Strategy

Strategy is defined as actions managers—which, in this context, include both senior managers and oversight governing boards—take to attain a firm's objectives. Academic institutions have different objectives, and priorities differ according to market conditions, customer preferences, and competitive factors.

Strategies may be viewed in the context of its formation or execution (Kaplan & Neimhocker, 2003; Thorpe & Morgan, 2007). It is impacted by factors such as problem perception and rationalization, context, culture and process, structure, level of control, leadership, and communication (Drazin & Howard, 1984; Jaworski et al., 1993; Nutt, 1983; Simon, 1996; Wall & Wall, 1995; Workman, 1993).

In strategy development, planning is key. In fact, the cornerstone of many academic institutions is the Strategic Plan. The plan that the institution envisions and implements determines success. Planning entails the establishment of goals, as well as the identification of necessary resources in order that goals will be achieved. Planning generates positive organizational results and can lead to financial gains (Berman et al., 1997; Schwenk & Shrader, 1993).

Leadership is equally important since it determines how and when the plans are executed. It also involves collaborating with multiple stakeholders and is a social process (Day, 2001). Responsible leadership means involving others in the decision making process (Waldman & Siegel, 2008). Collaboration is a salient ingredient in strategic leadership (Mittal & Dorfman, 2012). It is anchored on results. Consequently, leadership approaches influence followers conduct relating to work, attitudes, and performance (Liden et al., 2014).

This book highlights the best practices in planning and leading academic institutions in a strategic context.

Book Organization

In this book, the authors offer a range of topics that are deemed relevant to contemporary university management. The management functions of Planning and Leading are emphasized. The intent is to provide tools for academic leaders to transform, reinvigorate, and even turn-around educational institutions.

Strategies in University Management (Volume 1) is organized into four sections. Section I is the **Introduction**. Section II is about **Planning for Success** and includes the following chapters: Raising academic quality: A playbook (*Fr. Dennis Holtschneider*), Using accreditation to create and sustain an institutional vision and effective planning (*Ralph Wolff*), Developing, managing, and measuring a fluid strategic action model for higher education (*Gary Bonvillian*), Effective communication to improve the quality of university instruction (*Ernesto Schiefelbein and Noel McGinn*), Going online: Pitfalls and best practices in distance education (*Mac Powell*), Leading comprehensive internationalization on campus (*Thimios Zaharopoulos*), Global higher education: A perspective from Spain (*Fernando Galvan*). Section III pertains to **Leading the Way** with chapters such as Never alone: Building an effective management team (*Gary Dill*), Creating and sustaining the university leadership pipeline (*Don Betz*), Managing diversity as a university strategy (*Geetha Garib*), and Managing duty of care obligations in a university setting (*Lisbeth Claus*). Section IV is the **Conclusion**.

A second volume of this book series in University Management covers the equally important management topics of **Organizing** and **Controlling**. It covers the subject of **Effective Organization** and includes the following chapters: Developing and maintaining meaningful relationships with faculty, staff, and students (*Arthur Kirk*); Optimizing the Board–President relationship: Best practices that make a difference (*Gene Habecker*); Pathways to entrepreneurship in the academe (*J. Mark Munoz*); Evaluating the impact of social networks on the university's public engagement (*Letizia Lo Presti and Vittoria Marino*); Business and academic linkages: The case of Georgia (*Kakha Shengalia and Shalva Machavariani*); and Quad-helix engagement for city and regional development: The role of universities in governance, leadership, and management (*Thandwa Mthembu*). There are also discussions on **Controlling for Success** with chapters such as: An empirical basis for strategic management of price and aid (*Richard Hesel and Craig Goebel*), Enrollment management (*Halia Valladares and David Docherty*), Assessment is everyone's business (*Wendy Weiner*), and Financial management in higher education (*Neal King and J. Mark Munoz*). Together, the two volumes provide a comprehensive perspective on the management of academic institutions and cover the four functions of management: Planning, Leading, Organizing, and Controlling.

Value Provided by Strategies

The authors and editors hope that through the essays provided, many educational institutions worldwide can be helped and revived. For those fortunate to be in a growth path, some of the innovative ideas featured in the book can provide a roadmap to sustainability and greater success.

This book is valuable to a diverse audience. The offered strategies are useful for: (1) University leaders and stakeholders—as they seek ways to revive their organizations and enhance its performance, (2) Management consultants—when they endeavor to help their clients find solutions to problems, (3) Administrators in government and international organizations—in their efforts to strengthen policies in education, (4) Private corporations—in their collaboration and partnership with colleges and universities, and (5) Educators and students—as they expand their knowledge on education in the 21st century.

A New Frontier for Academia

This book is a pioneering effort to converge the viewpoints of academic administrators and experts from around the world in order to identify the best potential strategies in university management. The book furthers the notion that strategic shift and innovative thinking is needed in contemporary academia. As a groundbreaking initiative in identifying strategies for success in university management, the editors, authors, and contributors of this book were confronted with the challenges and opportunities of embarking into a new frontier of knowledge. There were limited sources upon which to build this body of expertise, but there is an abundance of creative thinking to shape a new paradigm. It is our hope that this effort stimulates interest on the subject and paves the way for dynamic ideas for university management in the future.

References

Arambewela, R. (2010). Student experience in the globalized higher education market: Challenges and research imperatives. In F. Maringe and N. Foskett (Eds.) *Globalization and Internationalization in Higher Education: Theoretical, Strategic and Management Perspectives* (pp. 155–173). London: Continuum International.

Berman, J.A., Gordon, D.D., & Sussman, G. (1997). A study to determine the benefits small business firms derive from sophisticated planning versus less sophisticated types of planning. *The Journal of Business and Economic Studies, 3*(3), 1–11.

Day, D.V. (2001). Leadership development: A review in context. *Leadership Quarterly, 11,* 581–613.

Denneen, J., & Dretler, T. (2012). The financially sustainable university. Accessed March 16, 2015. Viewable at: http://www.bain.com /publications/articles/financially-sustainable-university.aspx

Drazin, R., & Howard, P. (1984). Strategy implementation: A technique for organizational design. *Columbia Journal of World Business, 19*(Summer), 40–46.

English, L.M., Guthrie, J., & Parker, L.D. (2005). Recent public sector financial management change in Australia: Implementing the market model. In J. Guthrie, C. Humphrey, L.R. Jones, and O. Olson (Eds.) *International Public Financial Management Reform: Progress, Contradictions, and Challenges* (pp. 23–54). Connecticut: Information Age.

Jaworski, B.J., Stathakopoulos, V., & Krishnan, H.S. (1993). Control combinations in marketing: conceptual framework and empirical evidence. *Journal of Marketing, 57*(1), 406–419.

Kaplan, S., & Neimhocker, E.D. (2003). The real value of strategic planning. *Sloan Management Review, 44*(2), 71–76.

Liden, R.C., Panaccio, A., Meuser, J.D., Hu, J., & Wayne, S.J. (2014). Servant leadership: Antecedents, processes, and outcomes. In D.V. Day (Ed.) *The Oxford Handbook of Leadership and Organizations* (pp. 357–379). Oxford, England: Oxford University Press.

Lomas, L. (2002). Does the development of mass education necessarily mean the end of quality? *Quality in Higher Education, 8*(1), 71–79.

Mittal, R., & Dorfman, P.W. (2012). Servant leadership across cultures. *Journal of World Business, 47,* 555–570.

McDonald, M. (2014). Small US colleges battle death spiral as enrollment drops. Accessed on October 21, 2014. Viewable at: http://www.bloomberg.com/news/2014-04-14/small-u-s-colleges-battle-death-spiral-as-enrollment-drops.html

Nutt, P.C. (1983). Implementation approaches for project planning. *Academy of Management Review, 8*(4), 600–611.

Rytmeister, C. (2009). Governing university strategy; perceptions and practice of governance and management roles. *Tertiary Education & Management, 15*(2), 137–156.

Schwenk, C.R., & Shrader, C.B. (1993). Effects of formal strategic planning on financial performance in small firms: A meta-analysis. *Entrepreneurship Theory and Practice Spring,* 53–64.

Simon, H. (1996). *The Sciences of the Artificial,* 3rd ed. Boston, MA: MIT Press.

Thorpe, E.R., & Morgan, R.E. (2007). In pursuit of the 'ideal approach' to successful marketing strategy implementation. *European Journal of Marketing, 41*(5/6), 659–677.

Waldman, D.A., & Siegel, D. (2008). Defining the socially responsible leader. *Leadership Quarterly, 19,* 117–131.

Wall, S.J., & Wall, S.R. (1995). The evolution (not the death) of strategy. *Organizational Dynamics, 24,* 7–19.

Willson, C., Negoi, R., & Bhatnagar, A.S. (2010). University risk management. *Internal Auditor,* August, 65–68.

Workman, J.P. (1993). Marketing's limited role in new product development in one computer systems firm. *Journal of Marketing Research, 30,* 405–421.

Part 1

Planning for Success

CHAPTER 2

Raising Academic Quality: A Playbook

Rev. Dennis H. Holtschneider, CM

Universities compete in numerous ways, including the mix of academic programs they offer, their price, location, support services, and any number of amenities. They compete, too, on the impression and reality of the quality of the education being conveyed.

Repositioning an institution's "academic quality" is a challenging task. It requires financial investments, to be sure. It also requires the imagination and commitment of administrators and faculty to change their current practice in meaningful ways. It requires, too, a certain combination of intellectual substance and reputational work.

Tactical Vagueness

In truth, the term "academic quality" is often loosely coupled to actual student learning, referring more to the broad array of inputs and activities as well as outcomes that may more often pertain to individuals than the student body as a whole. There are at least three reasons for this.

First, student learning turns out to be harder to define and measure than many education reformers would care to admit. If the purpose of a business education is to compute net present value accurately, then measurement is simple. If it is to prepare a student to successfully identify business opportunities and then start and run a business, that will reveal itself only in time and may only partially be explainable by the education received. If, however, the purpose of a "quality" higher education includes noble citizenship and various claims for virtue, counting how many students took part in service activities hardly suffices.

But what if a "quality education" is defined by the immediacy of job placement upon graduation, or the starting salaries; or how far graduates rise in their fields over time or earn over time? Are those sufficient marks of an educated person? Are they truly markers of the value-added contribution of the education process if they are also inextricable from the advantages of birth into wealthy families and connected communities of privilege? Are these outcomes even fully under the control of the institution, or controlled by the ever shifting economy?

Second, while activities to raise academic quality are undertaken out of concern for student learning, they are just as often undertaken to draw a wealthier clientele who can pay the increasing costs of higher education, or to better secure market share in hotly contested regions by being perceived as a stronger institution than the one nearby.

More importantly, claims of academic quality and prestige are high-stakes assertions for institutions and for the presidents who lead them. What school could withstand a general public perception that their academic quality was poor or had declined in a measurable way? What president could possibly assert anything other than his or her school was "above-average?"

University administrators often avoid, therefore, explaining the true reasons for academic quality initiatives. Candid conversations about what constitutes academic "quality" can stir up controversy and slow a university community's readiness to pursue the projects being proposed. They can contradict and compromise the marketing efforts of the admissions staff. They can also lead to calls for measurement of actual student learning, something both faculty and administrators fear being held accountable for when the measurements are notoriously difficult to devise.

Rather, when universities propose activities to reposition the institution, the advantages to the institution are simply taken as self-evident, and if anything, portrayed as bettering an already satisfactory situation. Tactically, a certain vagueness enables institutions to get on with various initiatives. The challenge, of course, is for an institution to be honest with itself, if not with its various publics, as to the quality concerns to be addressed and improved and then to choose initiatives that directly accomplish those goals.

Sticker Price and Selectivity

Which men's suit is better quality: the one costing $800 or the $1,600? One would hope the shopper knows to how and why to pinch the lining, to note the buttons and stitching, and to recognize fine fabric. For the ordinary shopper, however, the price itself is the quality indicator most relied upon.

To a degree, the same is true for higher education. Admissions professionals have long attracted applications using a "high-tuition-high-aid" strategy, where a sticker price is set substantially above the actual cost to drive perceptions of quality, and then offset with tuition discounts characterized as "scholarships." There are multiple reasons for this, but it begins with a long proven observation that, when it comes to higher education, the market desires a high-priced product more than the low-cost option.

Universities take advantage of this dynamic to create a quality impression that will attract a stronger student body with higher SAT scores or from better quality high schools. To the degree they are successful, faculty find they can teach more easily, introduce more challenging material at a faster clip, reduce the time they spend correcting poor writing skills, and rely on the students themselves to raise the caliber of classroom discussion. The strategy is to create a stronger educational experience in time by creating an impression of rising standards.

Not dissimilarly, institutions are known to "announce" that they are raising their entry standards in an effort to set an impression of the institution's quality and desirability, hoping to attract a stronger cohort of students. Or, by increasing applications while holding the size of the freshman class constant, broadcasting that the selectivity of the institution has increased. The hope is that high school counselors will take notice and encourage stronger applicants in their directions in future years.

As any bell-curve might suggest, the numbers of potential students are progressively smaller as scores rise, and increasingly sought by many universities. An institution may find itself having to discount these students deeply to get them to attend or having to broaden one's traditional recruiting region by hiring additional recruiters and investing in marketing activities within those new regions. There is a classic cost-benefit tradeoff that admissions departments must eventually acknowledge.

To moderate the risk, schools sometimes provide "side doors" to admit students with lesser admission qualifications, and then do not report their test scores to government and ranking surveys. Spring enrollment, evening programs, opportunity programs, or even welcoming students "provisionally" enable schools to siphon some students away from the traditional freshman class and then report higher average freshman student entry qualifications, while continuing to accept students with a lower profile. These practices border on the untruthful, but are well known in American higher education.

More straightforwardly, institutions may raise their reported entry standards by building or expanding academic programs that are known to attract a higher caliber of students and perhaps even students with higher abilities to pay non-discounted tuition, such as pre-medical and other health-related majors.

As attractive and conceptually elegant as these strategies might be, their effect is modest at best. As more universities go to the "common app" to generate additional applications that can be denied, any early "statistical advantage" is lost. High school advisors are sophisticated enough to track who among their students were accepted and were not and to share actual "entry standards" information among their peers.

And so which is it? Must an institution first raise its academic quality to enable it to command a higher price? Or will the market's simplistic judgments about quality allow an institution to raise its price and then take the resulting increased income and invest it smartly to create the quality institution it portrayed through its pricing scheme? Kalsbeek and Zucker insist it is mostly the former.[1] A university's "net revenue per student" is largely set by the market, and the impressions that market has of the institution compared with its competitors. Setting the shortcuts aside, then, the trick is to invest and improve some set of quality indicators that matter to a defined market.

Faculty Hiring and Development

Leadership matters. For a president or provost, the most effective single tactic to raise a college's academic quality is to appoint a wise and

---

[1] Kalsbeek, D.H., & Zucker, B. (2014). Market and market niches. In D. Hossler, B. Bontrager, and associates (Eds.) *Handbook of Strategic Enrollment Management* (pp. 77–102). San Francisco: Jossey-Bass.

knowledgeable dean or department chair who has taken the task to heart. New leadership over a unit breaks open both a conversation and expectation of change in a way few other moves engender.

Similarly, faculty hiring is the most immediately substantive method to supplement the breadth and depth of expertise within a given program, assuming, of course, that the faculty are personally committed to building the program.

Whether dean or faculty, the difference maker is if the individual treats the position as a "start-up" business, of sorts. New leaders and colleagues bring fresh ideas, new connections and new energy to the entire group. The challenge is always the human factor.

This is particularly true when hiring "academic stars" to raise a program's quality. Academic stars can settle into their own projects and do little for the larger enterprise, unless their role is discussed clearly at the outset. Renowned new hires can be "marketed" in their own right to recruit stronger students and faculty. They can attract third-party funding, and they can mentor and bring young faculty into important research and professional worlds. They can also use their privileged roles on academic journal editorial boards, academic association leadership, and/or conference-organizing committees to further bring the department into major intellectual work of the moment. They can even add a bit to the department's overall competitive spirit, hopefully raising everyone's game. The reduced teaching loads and other arrangements made to recruit them can feed professional jealousy, however, and sometimes confound departmental cohesion. Any strategy of introducing a "star" into the department's midst has to be handled with sensitivity.

Whether or not new hiring is an option, investments in current faculty also can have a strong effect on elevating a program, giving faculty time and resources to update and retool, build key international relationships, consult or otherwise practice their craft for a time, visit competing institutions, and see fresh ideas at work. The classic sabbatical leave of offering time to read and reflect through their own writing, if well-planned, remains a powerful way for faculty to update and broaden their knowledge in a given field, or to strategically shift toward a new specialization. More creative forms of leave also can be helpful. Performance-based faculty can be given time away to tour, or more flexible schedules during the academic year. Scientists can be sent to spend time in labs with their colleagues elsewhere in the world. Faculty preparing students for specific professions can take time to work in those professions themselves and thereby build new contacts and update themselves on current practice.

When it comes to enhancing an academic program, not all research time or leaves are equally strategic. Some are more useful for the faculty member's expertise and development, and while that may serve its own purpose in keeping individual professors' teaching fresh in the classroom, administrators who want to leverage an institution must offer faculty larger opportunities to rebuild a unit or program, and give them the wherewithal to do so, including any knowledge base they require. The delicate conversation with faculty is to invite or approve leaves that serve the larger purpose, even as they serve the desired needs of the individual faculty member. Toward this end, many universities no longer grant sabbatical leaves automatically every 7 years, but instead ask faculty to propose a course of action and set of "deliverables" that will serve both them and the institution.

Most difficult, of all, however, are those situations where a given faculty member cannot or will not change his or her own practice or otherwise cooperate. In some cases, the department chair simply has to work around them, assigning workload that minimizes the impact of their intransigence. In the end, no program design can rise above what happens within a faculty member's classroom. The maxim "addition by subtraction" exists for a reason.

Curricular Rigor

The heart of any institution's educational quality is the outcome question on the day students graduate: "What do graduates know and what can they do because they spent time under our tutelage?" This is largely a question of curriculum.

Reforming a curriculum has been compared to moving a graveyard, and for good reason.[2] Challenging, difficult questions lie underneath,

---

[2] Zolner, J. (1996). Moving the academic graveyard: The dynamics of curricular change. *Selections*, Winter, 1–10.

such as "What should students know?" and "How will we know if they know it?" All too human dynamics surface as well, even to the point of faculty simply finding a comfort and appreciation for the status quo.

Among the newer for-profit institutions and even within some more traditional community colleges, the rigor and content of curriculum are determined centrally, either with content experts to design courses or using groups of expert faculty to set standards together. Courses are then offered using these central standards, and faculty are expected to adhere to these protocols as a way in which the larger institution can better "guarantee" a certain educational outcome.

Most universities eschew this approach, trusting the individual faculty themselves, as professionals, to design courses of sufficient caliber and content to reasonably prepare students to be conversant and capable in the material they are studying. Calibration of the proper level of rigor comes over time as faculty see the capability of the given student body that has been recruited to the institution, but also from conversations with other faculty as they compare syllabi and settle in to a given level of rigor.

The challenge of this approach is immediately evident. Students studying freshman writing with one professor may encounter startlingly challenging standards of grammar, syntax, and form, whereas students in another class may receive a single grade at the top of a paper with little or no feedback. One professor may be lecturing on the latest decisions of the Federal Reserve's economic policies, whereas another is reading from the dusty notes of a macrofinance lecture written years earlier.

Institutions that wish to increase rigor, update content, or create a more consistent educational experience for all students generally must find ways to do so while honoring faculty professionalism and academic freedom. Perhaps the most common is simply when department chairs, individual faculty, or more senior administrators ask a leading question.

- "How does our curriculum compare to our peer institutions and the aspirational schools we all respect?"
- "What graduate programs accept or deny our graduates? How could our curriculum prepare them better?"
- "How has our field changed in recent years, and where in the curriculum is this being presented?"

- "What do recruiters say about our students, and how can we adjust our programs to make them more competitive?"

The use of external comparators is a useful and effective way that many administrators employ to raise questions that skate near the edge of faculty prerogative. Rather than introducing new standards or specific content, they bring eternal ideas to bear and then "call the question" of how the department should adjust given this external information. Some institutions set an aspiration of seeking a prestigious accreditation for their academic programs, and thereby invite on a regular basis an outside review that forces the curricular questions. Where accreditations do not exist, institutions sometimes arrange their own periodic external academic department reviews and invite experts from other institutions to visit and provide feedback. Others create more permanent advisory boards of experts who visit at least annually and ask penetrating questions that can push the department forward in important ways. Some universities improve their curricula by taking a close look at the training programs that legal firms and businesses establish because they do not trust the universities to have fully educated their newest employees. Liberal arts institutions seek Phi Beta Kappa membership, a jewel in any institution's crown, and yet another external set of goals that can galvanize an institution's self-transformation.

To the degree that these external advisors are truly recognized as experts, faculty are generally willing to be advised and even critiqued. It often helps, however, if the college or university administration connects this external feedback into its strategic planning, its annual budgeting, and its capital plans. Faculty will respect a process that will lead to investment in their program and that they believe will come to fruition. Over time, they will choose to pay it lip service or actually implement it depending on whether its outcomes have been incorporated into the institution's investments.

Some departments use students as a source of ideas for improvement. Besides taking course evaluations seriously, some departments create common examinations or develop assessment tools to measure student achievement, and then adjust their pedagogical techniques, time-on-task, and curricular substance accordingly.[3]

---

[3] Angelo, T.A., & Cross, K.P. (1993). *Classroom Assessment Techniques: A Handbook for College Teachers*, 2nd ed. San Francisco: Jossey-Bass, Inc.

Other departments will set common, specific, and measurable learning goals for courses and for entire programs. Many create public moments where students can display their mastery of the material in front of their peers, ranging from in-house research conferences, where history majors present their senior theses to faculty and students from the department, to taking students nationally and internationally to conferences in the field to present in student-tracks or to co-present with faculty themselves. Some have students who present business plans before real angel investors for funding, or compete in national challenges in a given field. To the degree that students distinguish themselves nationally, universities frequently use these successes for recruiting purposes.

At the lower end of the spectrum, some colleges will set or raise their minimum standards for entry into the major, recommendation for student teaching, professional certification, or for receiving recommendations for graduate school. Other institutions identify the courses that students fail most often and/or drop-out of the university after failing. Popularly known as "gateway courses," faculty will redesign the courses, so that more students master the material, or tighten the prerequirements so that they are suitably prepared.

Curricular improvement is necessarily a decentralized activity, and institutions often accept that the work and outcome will be uneven. Some departments will have higher standards for the students in their majors simply because the faculty are willing to ask the questions and make the adjustments. Some institutions, however, will seek to invest in and raise the quality of a limited number of academic units above the others by design. They may even focus a department on one school of thought or other specialization within a field, in order to build and lay claim to being among the finest in the country for that single specialization.

Ph.D. programs, particularly, bring luster to an institution, even if they normally must be subsidized by the other operations of the university. At times, institutions will seek to establish doctoral programs specifically to change the rankings classification of their institution from regional to national, or to create a public impression that because they offer the Ph.D., they are a better institution than in the past or than their present competitors. This strategy frequently requires extensive investment and an acceptance that these units will be more highly resourced than others in the institution.

Similarly, many institutions will institute an honors program or even honors college in order to attract a more capable student that might otherwise be bored with the institution-wide curriculum or with the general student body. Honors programs have numerous benefits for the students who enroll in them, but they are also used strategically. They enable a university to invest in students who, in turn, can achieve at a level that can be trumpeted by an institution, such as increased numbers of students accepted into medical school or law school for example, or increased numbers of students receiving Fulbright, Marshall, or perhaps even Rhodes scholarships. Institutions also hope that bringing in a brighter-than-average (and predictably wealthier-than-average) cohort of honors students will in time lead other similarly gifted students from other institutions to enroll and thereby raise the overall profile of the student body.[4]

Even where there is not an honors program, institutions find it useful to establish targeted advising for students who hope to attend graduate school, or who intend to apply for prestigious post-graduate opportunities. Again, institutions hope that by helping certain gifted students achieve at very high levels, they can attract larger cohorts of students who are seeking the same.

There are also any number of surveys that can provide internal and external benchmarking, and therefore help to drive change.[5]

The Company They Keep

Institutions frequently attempt to change the public's perception—and in turn, the reality—by increasing the distinction of the company they keep or the students they draw. Most commonly, this is seen in the aspiration for institutions to become a research intensive institution, and then to advance further along that continuum over time. "Colleges" will not infrequently re-brand themselves as "universities" for much the same reason.

---

[4] Selingo, J. (May 31, 2002). Mission Creep?: More regional state colleges start honors programs to raise their profiles and draw better students. *The Chronicle of Higher Education*.

[5] Ewell, P.T. (2006). *Making the Grade: How Boards Can Ensure Academic Quality* (pp. 60–62). Washington DC: AGB Press.

At other times, institutions will raise one specific program to levels of prestige far beyond the rest of the programs and then use that marquis program—and especially heightened comparator set that it commands—to bring reflected glory to the institution. Others, such as Rensselaer and OSU, will invest heavily in select areas of specialization for the same reason.[6]

Some specifically seek to join new athletic conferences, so that they can be associated in the public mind with the academic reputations of the other member schools. Some form international study abroad partnerships with prestigious institutions overseas—such as the renowned Lausanne Hotel School or the London School of Economics—and immediately raise the impression of the program's quality by association. Some partner for research with well-respected organizations, such as Pew or Merkt.

Others announce internship opportunities with highly respected firms, such as Google for IT students or Paramount Pictures for film students. Some invite guest speakers or executives-in-residence, such as Wynton Marsalis for jazz studies, or Toni Morrison for writing. Some might outsource and partner with well-known brands where learning could be improved or campus facilities are substandard, for example using Berlitz for foreign language instruction or a prominent school for culinary instruction.

Some institutions, however, start their journey toward improvement by standing out as unique against the field of competitors with whom they wish to be associated, becoming known nationally for their excellence in contradistinction to the rest for that particular item, and then, in time, taking a step back toward full-service but at a higher level. Northeastern University's co-op program, for example, helped it emerge from the tightly condensed pack in Boston. It then took that new attention, lessened their reliance on co-op self-definition, and pursued an aggressive rankings improvement strategy.[7]

Others jettison the part of the institution that holds them back in the public eye. Universities will close weaker programs and often shift resources to build stronger more competitive ones, such as Emory did when it closed its Journalism program.[8]

---

[6] "Shirley Ann Jackson Sticks to the Plan." *Chronicle of Higher Education.* June 15, 2007. http://www.dispatch.com/content/stories/local/2012/11/13/osu-faculty.html.
[7] Kutner, M. (September 2014). How to Game the College Rankings: Northeastern University's single-minded focus on just one list. *Boston Magazine.*
[8] http://news.emory.edu/stories/2012/09/EmoryCollegePlan/campus.html.

The same principle holds when universities shift a less-prepared portion of their student body elsewhere. As Miami University of Ohio and The Ohio State University become increasingly selective, they are assigning lesser qualified students to the state's regional campuses, with the promise that they can transfer to the flagship campus later. The University of Florida is doing much the same using its online options and thereby repositioning the profile of the traditional student body.[9]

Shiny Objects

Universities have long sought to create powerful impressions of strength and quality using architecture. New or extensively renovated buildings and grounds can have a powerful lift effect on the impression one forms of a university. There are, in fact, many ways that universities invest to create a better impression that may or may not be related to the actual quality of the academics, but which can assist an institution to raise its reputation and, in turn, its quality.

Some institutions employ early adoption strategies to distinguish their institutions from the rest. Oftentimes, this involves bringing the latest technology onto the campus or into the educational process. At times, it can be as simple as slightly adjusting and renaming current degree programs to take advantage of popular concepts, such as "forensic" accounting, forensic law, forensic biology, and forensic chemistry in the 2000s, or the breadth of "sustainability" studies in the 2010s.[10]

Universities create their own prizes and medals to honor the best in a given field, and share. Harvard University, for example, awards the national W.E.B. DuBois Medal for contributions to African American Culture and the life of the mind.[11] The Iowa Short Fiction Prize is awarded by the University of Iowa Writers' Workshop. Columbia University annually awards the Pulitzer Prize.

Similarly, universities trumpet an endless parade of awards from accounting competitions, magazine rankings, and computer hacking competitions, all of which can assist an institution to raise its reputation.

---

[9] http://chronicle.com/blogs/ticker/u-of-florida-gets-few-takers-for-online-path-to-campus/99641.

[10] http://sspp.proquest.com/sspp_institutions/display/universityprograms.

[11] http://hutchinscenter.fas.harvard.edu/dubois/about/w-e-b-du-bois-medalists

Some find ways in which the campus name is associated with important social conversations. The first presidential debate is always held at St. Anselm College in New Hampshire. Quinnipiac University famously houses the Quinnipiac polls.[12] Other universities establish yearly lecture series or otherwise invite prominent individuals and scholars-in-residence whose comments will make news or can at least be pictured in the university's view book and social media, such as Supreme Court justices or High Point University's association with Steve Wozniak.[13]

Other institutions seek to participate in projects funded by prestigious foundations, whose reputation can burnish the university's own, such as MacArthur or Gates, or to participate in federal projects such as Civic Engagement Honor Roll.

All of these can serve as proof points and public relations opportunities that a given university is on the move and perhaps rising faster and higher than its traditional peers. Reputations change slowly and attempts to change popular opinion require constant feeding.

Observations

A decade ago, Elon University grabbed the nation's admiration for the way in which it successfully repositioned itself from a small, undistinguished regional institution, to a selective, national liberal arts institution. Independently examining how the university managed this, George Keller made clear that there was no magic bullet, but extensive, dogged work on many fronts, let by a stable, long-serving administration with the close collaboration of the faculty at every turn.[14] More recently, High Point University has attempted to follow a similar route, again demonstrating that a combination of many initiatives, centered most importantly on the actual quality of instruction and caliber of faculty, matters enormously.[15]

---

[12] http://www.quinnipiac.edu/news-and-events/quinnipiac-university-poll/

[13] http://www.highpoint.edu/president/2013/10/03/nido-qubein-steve-wozniak-video/

[14] Keller, G., & Lambert, L. (2014). *Transforming a College: The Little-Known College's Strategic Climb to National Distinction*. Baltimore: Johns Hopkins University Press.

[15] MacTaggart, T. (2007). The three stages of college and university revitalization. *Academic Turnarounds: Restoring Vitality to Challenged American Colleges and Universities* (pp. 3–18). Washington DC: American Council on Education/Praeger.

In both cases, fundraising played a key role. Growing the endowment or completing a capital campaign or deploying the income from unexpected athletic successes are not strategies themselves, but few plans of any ambition can be completed without bringing new resources to bear.

In both cases, however, the key work of improving the academic quality of the institution was accompanied by sophisticated and powerful strategies and also shifting the public perception of the institution. Some of these methods of shaping public perception border on sleight-of-hand if they are not accompanied by substantive increases in academic rigor. But when taken together, much like the classic chicken and egg question, both sets of activities smoothed and assisted the other. Some shifts, such as raising student entry standard, actually served both a substantive and a public relations function.[16]

The noble challenge amidst any of this activity is to remember and perhaps even protect the institution's mission of whom it was designed to serve. Employing these many strategies, it is far easier to pursue a strategy that seeks wealthier and more privileged students, replacing less-prepared and needier populations who once attended the institution. In truth, most institutions that consider themselves "elite" today serve only a small proportion of first-generation and underrepresented students. In a national context, where the "American Dream" remains as a national ideal, universities that seek distinction may wish to add the additional goal of doing so while continuing to provide a powerful pipeline for those whose families cannot afford such an education for their children. There is a typical playbook for universities to rise in distinction, but it may not always serve the public interest or the institution's historic mission.[17]

That challenge noted, students and their parents have asked us to show them the world and prepare them for it. There is a nobility to the task of raising an institution's academic rigor and substance, as it honors the request of those who entrust their education to our hands.

---

[16] Carlson, S. (November 14, 2010). "How to Build a Perception of Greatness: It's Hard to Bottle the Buzz about a Hot College, But These Suggestions Can Help." *The Chronicle of Higher Education.*

[17] Luzer, D. (August 22, 2010). "The Prestige Racket: George Washington University." *Washington Monthly.* http://www.washingtonmonthly.com/college_guide/feature/the_prestige_racket.php?page=all. Keller, J. (March 7, 2010). "As Its Popular Chief Retires, USC Seeks an Encore." *The Chronicle of Higher Education.*

CHAPTER 3

Using Accreditation to Create and Sustain an Institutional Vision and Effective Planning

Ralph A. Wolff

Planning is bringing the future into the present so that you can do something with it now.

—Alan Lakein

Accreditation is an episodic process that can be used effectively to engage multiple constituencies toward a new or more effective institutional vision. Such a new vision can then drive institutional planning and management. This chapter explores how to move beyond a compliance mentality with accreditation toward engaging accreditation standards through the self-study process to revitalize an institutional mission, draw constituent groups together, and gain external affirmation from the evaluation team of the directions the institution has developed.

Higher education is in an era of dramatic change. Financial, technological, and enrollment challenges have created an environment where it is not certain that all institutions—public or private—will be able to thrive, let alone survive in the future. The recent decision to close Sweet Briar College (notwithstanding its reopening) reflects the pressures that many small colleges currently face. Public institutions no longer can count on sufficient levels of state support to maintain affordable tuition costs for students, as reflected by the elimination of all state funding for two Arizona Community Colleges. Even for those institutions that seem to be faring well, serious questions are being repeatedly raised whether college is worth the cost (Bennett & Wilezol, 2013), whether students are actually achieving significant learning gains in college (Arum & Roksa, 2011), and whether graduates are well prepared for today's and tomorrow's workplace (Grasgreen, 2013).

Realistic visioning and planning in this dynamic environment may be *the* critical process that will enable institutions to navigate these changes. At any given moment in time, institutions have multiple plans in place, at multiple levels within the institution. Rarely, however, are they coordinated or their effectiveness regularly monitored with targeted outcomes, metrics, and milestones. Most institutions undergo strategic planning periodically, typically at the end of previous planning cycles and often soon after a new president arrives. Little understood is how institutional accreditation can (and should) be used as a major tool both to set an institutional vision and to undertake (or evaluate) the effectiveness of planning across the institution.

Accreditation[1] is a substantial multiyear process that all institutions of higher education periodically undergo. While accreditation historically developed as a voluntary process undertaken through associations of schools and colleges, it has now become essential for linkage to federal (and state) financial aid, and acceptance of credit awards and degrees. Organized into six regions (and seven accrediting commissions[2]), over 3,000 institutions are now accredited by the regional accrediting bodies.

It involves a comprehensive self-study, followed by a site team visit and an accrediting agency action. All too frequently, however, it is seen as a necessary burden primarily to demonstrate conformity to the standards of the accrediting agency, rather than an opportunity to scan the future and create (or renew) an institutional vision and strategic goals, along with planning processes that will pull the institution forward in this era of significant change.

In the course of my work as president of an accrediting agency, I found that nearly all decision letters commented on some element of institutional

---

[1] In this chapter, accreditation refers to institutional accreditation as undertaken by the regional accrediting commissions.

[2] The Western Association is unique, being divided into community college and senior college commissions.

planning, and the majority of these letters contained recommendations for the institution to improve or undertake some dimension of planning. To assess the currency of this observation, I undertook a review of recent actions taken by the WASC Senior College and University Commission (2015) in June 2014 as reflected in the Commission's decision letters since they are public. Using a sample of 12 actions, all identified planning as a key issue that led up to the current accrediting review or were cited in the decision letter as an area in need of further improvement. Given that not all accrediting standards were cited in these letters, that all letters cited planning in one fashion or another highlights its centrality to accreditation and institutional effectiveness. In this sample, seven institutions were praised for progress made in planning. At the same time, however, 6 of this group were still charged to improve one or more dimensions of planning as an area of follow-up, and 9 of the 12 institutions overall were called upon to improve planning efforts.

In light of the frequency with which accreditation cites planning as an area in need of improvement or further development, it is useful to consider the ways in which accrediting agencies approach planning and define their expectations. All seven regional commissions have a set of standards regarding multiple aspects of planning. In this regard, accrediting standards identify a number of key components of planning:

1. A clear vision for the future
2. A strategic plan and planning processes to identify key goals and priorities
3. Academic planning processes leading to an academic plan
4. Enrollment plans
5. Financial plans
6. Technology plans
7. Human resource plans
8. Physical facility and deferred maintenance plans

Agencies tie together these several types of plans by calling for integrated and/or comprehensive plans and planning processes. Agencies also expect planning to be ongoing across all departments, academic, co-curricular, and nonacademic. In addition, planning is expected to be evidence-based, data-driven, and tracked over time. These are further described below.

The core principle of accreditation is that quality is mission driven, which allows for the rich diversity of institutions operating in the United States—ranging from highly selective to open access, research-centered to comprehensive teaching centered, and faith-based to specialized colleges and universities. Central to the accrediting process, therefore, is the clarity and integration of the institution's mission in all institutional operations. This is reflected in the standards of all accrediting agencies. For example, Criterion One of the Higher Learning Commission (2015) (HLC) states: "The institution's mission is clear and articulated publicly; it guides the institution's operations." Similarly, the Southern Association of Colleges and Schools (SACS) states in Standard 3.1.1:

> The mission statement is current and comprehensive, accurately guides the institution's operations, is periodically reviewed and updated, is approved by the governing board, and is communicated to the institution's constituencies.

While mission statements are required for accreditation, they can be static, even historical, documents. Building on the mission statement, vision statements and strategic plans chart the direction of the institution and define how to engage the many forces impacting the institution. As stated by the New England Association of Schools and Colleges (2011), "The institution's mission provides the basis upon which the institution identifies its priorities, plans its future and evaluates its endeavors; it provides a basis for the evaluation of the institution against the Commission's Standards."

Flowing from the centrality of the institution's mission is the need for a vision for the institution for the future. Does the vision statement articulate a vision for what the institution is becoming in this era of change? Does it provide an inspiring as well as achievable portrait? In *Turnaround*, Sandra Elman (p. 158), president of the Northwest Commission on College and Universities (2010), cites creating a vision to sustain institutional identify as a key task for an effective self-study, especially for financially struggling institutions. This is the case today for all institutions. Reassessing the vision for the institution is a valuable exercise for all institutions. Because self-studies necessarily engage a cross section of stakeholders within an institution, the process becomes a valuable vehicle for reaffirming the future direction or identifying areas of needed change.

Vision statements are typically tied to strategic planning, a vision statement identifies where the institution sees itself in the future; a strategic plan identifies the goals and priorities to achieve that vision. For example, NEASC Standard 2.3 calls for strategic planning: "The institution plans beyond a short-term horizon, including strategic planning that involves realistic analyses of internal and external opportunities and constraints." WASC (Senior) Standard 4.6 similarly states "[Planning] processes assess the institution's position, articulate priorities, examine the alignment of its purposes, core functions, and resources, and define the future direction of the institution." HLC Standard 5.C/3 carries this theme as well: "The planning process encompasses the institution as a whole...."

Planning is expected to occur across and throughout the institution, including academic, co-curricular, and support units of the institution. SACS states this well:

3.3.1   *The institution identifies expected outcomes, assesses the extent to which it achieves these outcomes, and provides evidence of improvement based on analysis of the results in each of the following areas:*

Institutional Effectiveness

3.3.1.1   *educational programs, to include student learning outcomes*
3.3.1.2   *administrative support services*
3.3.1.3   *academic and student support services*
3.3.1.4   *research within its mission, if appropriate*
3.3.1.5   *community/public service within its mission, if appropriate*

Planning is also expected to assure both the currency and the effectiveness of academic programs, and build on evidence from student learning outcomes assessments that demonstrate that students are

achieving intended learning outcomes. With increased emphasis in recent years on the assessment of student learning outcomes as a key part
of the accrediting process, the linkage of outcomes data to academic and
institutional planning has become all the more important. NEASC
Standard 2.5 states (in part): "[The institution's] system of evaluation is
designed to provide relevant and trustworthy information to support
institutional improvement, with an emphasis on the academic program." The academic strategic plan should drive the campus master plan
and financial and facilities planning, and address such issues as future
enrollment patterns, faculty growth, uses of technology (distance learning and learning management systems), and support services (Hallowell
& Middaugh, 2006, pp. 53–54).

HLC places emphasis in the linkage to student outcomes data in its
Standard 5.C.2: "The institution links its processes for assessment of student learning, evaluation of operations, planning, and budgeting." Accreditation Council for Community and Junior Colleges (2014) (ACCJC)
identifies this as a central focus of institutional planning and evaluation
"The institution demonstrates its effectiveness by providing 1) evidence of
the achievement of student learning outcomes and 2) evidence of institution and program performance. The institution uses ongoing and systematic
evaluation and planning to refine its key processes and improve student
learning." WASC (Senior) states this focus in Standard 4.6: "Assessment of
teaching, learning, and the campus environment—in support of academic
and co-curricular objectives—is undertaken, used for improvement, and
incorporated into institutional planning processes."

Planning also needs to include resource planning for future staffing,
technology, and facilities. Middle States Commission on Higher Education (2014) (MSCHE) identifies this area well in its Criteria under Standard 6: "fiscal and human resources as well as the physical and technical
infrastructure adequate to support its operations wherever and however
programs are delivered; ... and. comprehensive planning for facilities,
infrastructure, and technology that includes consideration of sustainability
and deferred maintenance and is linked to the institution's strategic and
financial planning processes...." NEASC identifies a similar theme in its
Standards 2.7: "Based on verifiable information, the institution understands what its students have gained as a result of their education and has

useful evidence about the success of its recent graduates. This information is used for planning and resource allocation and to inform the public about the institution."

Critical to the effectiveness of the multiple dimensions of planning is financial planning and the alignment and allocation of financial resources to fulfill these plans at multiple levels. HLC Standard 5.C.1 states this clearly: "1. The institution allocates its resources in alignment with its mission and priorities." MSCHE states, in the Criteria under Standard 6: "a financial planning and budgeting process that is aligned with the institution's mission and goals, evidence-based, and clearly linked to the institution's and units' strategic plans/objectives.... WASC (Senior) Standard 4.6 addresses this topic as follows: These processes assess the institution's position, articulate priorities, examine the alignment of its purposes, core functions, and resources, and define the future direction of the institution."

Planning is also expected to be participatory, and include key stakeholders inside and outside the institution. NWCCU Standard 3.A.2 characterizes this common theme across all agency standards: 3.A.2 The institution's comprehensive planning process is broad-based and offers opportunities for input by appropriate constituencies. WASC (Senior) Standard 4.5 identifies a range of stakeholders to be included: "Appropriate stakeholders, including alumni, employers, practitioners, students, and others designated by the institution, are regularly involved in the assessment and alignment of educational programs."

Increasingly planning needs to be based on data derived from effective institutional research. This is a theme running across all agency standards. WASC (Senior) states this directly in Standard 4.2: "The institution has institutional research capacity consistent with its purposes and characteristics. Data are disseminated internally and externally in a timely manner, and analyzed, interpreted, and incorporated in institutional review, planning, and decision-making. Periodic reviews are conducted to ensure the effectiveness of the institutional research function and the suitability and usefulness of the data generated." NWCCU states this expectation as well in Standard 4A: "The institution engages in ongoing systematic collection and analysis of meaningful, assessable, and verifiable data—quantitative and/or qualitative, as appropriate to its indicators of achievement—as the basis for evaluating the accomplishment of its core theme objectives."

In light of the multiple planning activities undertaken by institutions, reflected in these agency standards, there is the expectation that institutions periodically evaluate the effectiveness of their planning processes, and the resulting plans. This too is reflected in agency standards. NEASC states this in its Standard 2.8: "The institution determines the effectiveness of its planning and evaluation activities on an ongoing basis. Results of these activities are used to further enhance the institution's implementation of its purposes and objectives." ACCJC states this as well in Standard 2.6: "The institution assures the effectiveness of its ongoing planning and resource allocation processes by systematically reviewing and modifying, as appropriate, all parts of the cycle, including institutional and other research efforts."

One forward looking element in many of the agency's standards is using planning to address the many technology, demographic, and other changes impacting higher education. At WASC (Senior) this has been characterized as addressing the "changing ecology of higher education." In its Standard 4, this theme is embodied in Standard 4.7: "Within the context of its mission and structural and financial realities, the institution considers changes that are currently taking place and are anticipated to take place within the institution and higher education environment as part of its planning, new program development, and resource allocation." HLC strikes a similar theme in its Standard 5.C.5: "5. Institutional planning anticipates emerging factors, such as technology, demographic shifts, and globalization."

Notwithstanding the extensive set of agency standards laying out the multiple dimensions of planning expected of institutions, there are many pitfalls found by visiting teams as reflected in the survey cited above and personal experience. These include:

- Plans that have too many recommendations to be achieved in a reasonable timeframe, with no priorities being set
- Plans that are "wish lists" without grounding in evidence and data or clear priorities and goals
- Plans disconnected from a vision of the future direction of the institution, with different units having plans that are not aligned with the institution's strategic plan and vision

- Plans without a clear set of metrics to measure achievement or milestones to assess progress
- Plans without a clear person or committee assigned to monitor progress
- Plans disconnected from financial resources available to fulfill the goals, priorities, and recommendations
- Plans setting targets disconnected from actual enrollment, retention, and completion data
- Plans that have not involved broad consultation and involvement, or have not been communicated well back to these same constituencies
- Lack of sustained leadership for planning
- Lack of follow-through in implementing plans
- Personnel changes or intervening events that lead to ignoring or setting aside previously developed plans without effective communication

As is evident from the foregoing analysis, planning plays a central role in all accrediting agency standards and reviews. And notwithstanding the extensive detail in each agency's standards regarding planning, problems with planning are still found by peer review teams, leading to required follow-up citations by accrediting commissions. The accrediting process is built on institutional self-study and this process can and should be used to review the multiple dimensions of planning reflected in these standards. In so doing, the self-study can be used to engage multiple constituencies it and to move an institution toward a new vision and establish strategic goals. Planning the self-study with this goal in mind is a critical step, for example, by using the process to ask such questions across the institution as: "do we have a clear vision for the future that is effective; are we achieving our strategic goals and priorities (and do you even know what they are); does your unit have a clear plan that is driving resource allocations and behavior; do planning processes include all the needed stakeholders?"

Using such an inquiry approach creates an environment for candor, provides feedback from throughout the institution, and lays a foundation for future planning. Indeed, based on preliminary surveys of this sort, the self-study process itself could be used to create a new vision statement, or used to revise the strategic plan, etc. Such feedback is invaluable for institutional administration at all levels.

More important is to get ahead of these issues and plan, well ahead of the self-study, to review the timeframe of existing plans and planning processes and determine whether to use the self-study for strategic or academic planning, or to undertake these processes before the self-study and use the self-study to assess progress, establish monitoring mechanisms, etc. In this way, rather than the self-study being externally driven to satisfy an external accreditor, it can become a key management and planning tool in its own right. In conceiving of the self-study this way, there are significant virtues—it uses human capital wisely, aligns processes and avoids duplicative efforts, and reduces costs.

Substantial human capital is involved in the many layers and types of planning typically occurring throughout an institution—strategic visioning and planning, academic planning, financial planning, enrollment planning, technology planning, facilities (and deferred maintenance) planning, faculty and staff planning, and more. Given the many pitfalls that can, and often do occur, in the course of institutional planning, periodic assessment through the accrediting process can make a significant contribution to the institution. Because accrediting reviews are periodic, are mandatory, and emphasize planning in all their multiple dimensions, they provide an excellent framework for institutional reflection, evaluation, and future thinking. They are worth conceiving of the self-study and peer review as a value-adding enterprise that can serve to help any institution plan more effectively.

References

Accreditation Council for Community and Junior Colleges. (2014). *Accreditation Standards*. [data file]. Retrieved from accjc.org.

Arum, R., & Roksa, J. (2011). *Academically Adrift: Limited Learning on College Campuses*. Chicago: University of Chicago Press.

Bennett, W., & Wilezol, D. (2013). Is college worth it?: *A former United States Secretary of Education and a liberal arts graduate expose the broken promise of higher education*. Nashville: Thomas Nelson.

Elman, S. (2009). *Accreditation, Fragility, and Disclosure. In Turnaround: Leading Stressed Colleges and Universities to Excellence.* Baltimore: The Johns Hopkins University Press.

Grasgreen, A. (2013, October 29). *Qualified in Their Own Minds.* Retrieved from www.InsideHigherEd.com.

Higher Learning Commission. (2015). *The Criteria for Accreditation and Core Components.* Retrieved from www.hlcommission.org.

Hollowell, D., & Middaugh, M. (2006). *Integrating Higher Education Planning and Assessment: A Practical Guide.* Ann Arbor, MI: Society for College and University Planning.

Martin, Samuels & Associates. (2009). *Turnaround: Leading Stressed Colleges and Universities to Excellence.* Baltimore: The Johns Hopkins University Press.

Middle States Commission on Higher Education. (2014). *Standards for Accreditation and Requirements of Affiliation.* Retrieved from msche.org.

New England Association of Schools and Colleges. (2011). *Standards.* Retrieved from neasc.org.

Northwest Commission on Colleges and Universities. (2010). *Standards for Accreditation.* Retrieved from nwccu.org.

Smith, A. (2015, March 12). *Zeroed Out in Arizona.* Retrieved from www.InsideHigherEd.com.

Southern Association of Colleges and Schools Commission on Colleges. (2012). *The Principles of Accreditation: Foundations for Quality Enhancement.* Retrieved from http://www.sacscoc.org.

WASC Senior College and University Commission. (2015). *Accreditation Standards.* Retrieved from www.wascsenior.org.

CHAPTER 4

Developing, Managing, and Measuring a Fluid Strategic Action Model for Higher Education

Gary Bonvillian, Ph.D.

Introduction

Today's rapidly changing social, economic, and market forces present unprecedented challenges for higher education. In addition, there is a heightened demand for accountability and responsiveness coming from our state and national governments. These demands are real, frequent, and being linked to resources (Ward, 2013). At the same time, higher education is feeling increasing pressure from a discriminating public that has come to realize college and university options are considerable. In business terms, higher education is a buyers-market (Perez-Pena, 2014).

Today's reality is that colleges and universities must and will change the ways in which they operate to survive the day and better position themselves for long-term viability. Every president of a college or university, public or independent, is aware of the forces of change.

The alarm has been sounded over the past 30 years in a number of publications examining change in higher education (Bonvillian & Murphy, 1996; Boyer, 1987; Breneman, 1994; Clark, 1992; Keller, 1983). Some respond more effectively than others. Historians are likely to point back to this time period in the evolution of higher education in the United States and reflect on just how much these forces of change have influenced the core societal role of colleges and universities and how they function (Thelin, 2011).

In spite of the pressures, there is a case to be made that some colleges and universities have not only met the challenges well but also capitalized on them. These institutions have survived, and even thrived, in spite of what appears to be at times, insurmountable odds. This is particularly true in the small independent, not-for-profit, sector of higher education and even more so within those institutions that have never relied on public funds or endowments to fall back on during difficult times. In fact, a close examination of these institutions would reveal that the notion of responding to profound forces of change is not a new idea at all. These institutions have not only understood the challenge of change, they have embraced it for much of their existence. They have evolved as the forces have compelled them to do so. Had they not, the landscape of higher education would look quite different today.

Forty years ago, there were predictions that most small independent, not-for-profit schools would be closed or absorbed by now for lack of a critical mass of students (Astin & Lee, 1974). It did not happen and, in fact, there are hundreds of such colleges and universities in the United States today that make up this sector. Some have succumbed to the pressure and closed or merged, but the numbers that carry on are still great. The Council of Independent Colleges (2014) (CIC), a champion of independent colleges and universities since 1956, boasts a membership of nearly 750 schools, and this does not even include all the possible institutions in this sector.

Although higher education is steeped in traditions, astute leaders today have come to accept the fact that in order for their college or university to respond to the forces of change, they must employ many of the same principles of modern strategy and operations that might be found in virtually any business, industry, or even civic organization. At the center of successful organizational strategies today is the ability to structure operational goals and objectives that support the overarching longer term vision and mission, yet fluid enough to redirect resources if warranted. This is in contrast to the once held belief that organizations could establish long-term strategic planning models that did not account for the short-term impact of the forces of change and perhaps even missed opportunities presented as a result of those changes. The idea of rigid 5-year strategic plans has largely disappeared (Dooris, 2004). Who can predict the market 5 years out? We have difficulty predicting it 1 year out (Morrill, 2013).

There is certainly merit in embracing our past in higher education as that has played a large part in our growing role of importance in society. However, to most colleges and universities today it is responsiveness to the market, timely decision-making, efficient utilization of resources, and a continuous measuring of outcomes that lead to success.

This chapter describes a model for strategic action that is in use in one school with considerable success. Between 2006 and 2014, Thomas University (TU) grew from a mere 685 student headcount to over 1,100 in domestic programs and over 1,200 in the People's Republic of China (PRC); doubled its assets without expanding debt; nearly tripled its athletic program; more than doubled its programmable land holdings; and gained advances on its endowment.

The strategic model at TU incorporates an adaptation of *Hoshin Strategic Management* practices popularized in business and industry during the early years of our understanding of total quality principles.

This chapter describes the following:

- A description of the principles of this approach
- A leadership mandate at all levels of the organization
- A keen awareness of market demands
- An equal awareness of the college or university's capacity to act on threats and opportunities and ability to redirect resources
- A process for monitoring and measuring performance
- An example of the model in practice

Since the fall of 2006, TU has engaged in a dynamic action-oriented strategic initiative using a process that continuously looks to the future, yet is sensitive to the current core programs and processes essential to sustain the organization. A key element of this strategy approach is to understand and protect the core—those initiatives that have a proven performance record and perhaps have long carried the greatest load for assuring viability of the institution.

Adaptation of Hoshin Principles

Hoshin Strategic Management is a method of establishing, monitoring, and executing strategic priorities in a manner that allows for current operations to progress without disruption, while also engaging in continuous improvement and pursuing new breakthrough opportunities that show promise in supporting the overarching goals of the organization (Waldo, 2014).

This method for strategic action was originally employed at TU, in 2006, because of a compelling need to maintain successful on-going initiatives while also producing new and immediate (breakthrough) performance results directed toward enrollment growth and operational and financial stability. The current president has utilized this model in several schools as it is easily adapted to differing organizations. The following represents key guiding principles of TU's adaptation of the Hoshin principles into its own *Plan for Strategic Action*:

- Maintaining existing and successful initiatives that continue to carry or add value to the organization—TU understands what constitutes its core programs and primary revenue generating areas and does not allow them to be compromised as new opportunities are pursued
- Identifying breakthrough opportunities that can advance the organization to new levels of performance and incorporating them into the core—expanding the portfolio
- Continuous improvement of operating processes that assure strategic initiatives become operational reality—an uncompromising commitment to empower those in the best position to actually carry out the vision and the mission
- Continuous review of progress, with accountabilities for key leaders—a collaborative and routine exercise to hold each other accountable for results
- Remaining flexible enough to adjust priorities, if warranted—not being trapped by ill-considered plans and initiatives that fail to produce

The absence of wealth sharpens decision-making at colleges and universities such as TU as all resources are considered precious.

Leadership

Although it is widely accepted that successful strategic processes require engagement of all constituencies, ultimate responsibility for assuring progress of the school falls to the president. The president is the chief strategist. In the same respect, heads of major divisions must not only be involved in the formulation of that strategy but also are charged with actually carrying it out. At TU, the Administrative Team (A Team) is this body. The A Team's work is also reviewed and sanctioned by the Board of Trustees, who, according to by-laws, are the ultimate authority on strategy direction and are engaged at critical junctures in the process. Their role is not only to accept and approve the strategy but also to monitor progress.

The President is charged to present the Board of Trustees with a viable strategic model that assures the health of the university. He does this through a collaborative and collegial process of engagement with key constituents. This is not an unusual model for overseeing major institutional strategy and is considered essential by all regional accrediting bodies as well as scholars of higher education management (Beard, 2009; Morrill, 2013).

The total quality management lessons of the 1980s helped organizations discover that apparent sound strategy falls flat without an organization's ability to operationally carry it out. At TU that occurs in the divisions and departments. Visions and missions are merely words on paper and posters until they become reality through the working elements of the organization (Roberts, 1995; Seymour, 1992; Sims & Sims, 1995). At TU, the A Team, to include the President and key cabinet members, drives the strategy model. However, the handoff is swift to the operating units, which have considerable latitude in their execution to carry out the work that is directly linked back to the overarching strategic goals.

Market Demands

The notion of market pressures is hardly a new subject in higher education. Since the early 1980s, when the dynamic of markets changed for many colleges and universities, astute leaders became cognizant of the fact that higher education is a highly competitive enterprise. This gave rise to a new level of discussion of managing in higher education, to include emphasis on marketing (Keller, 1983). Although the demographics favored us, the competition was heating up. This competition was coming not only from within the public and independent sectors but also from the rapidly emerging proprietary colleges and universities. This latter element has grown to at least 3,000 institutions over the past 30 years (Association of Private Sector Colleges and Universities, 2015).

As a private university TU's tuition is high compared with the public colleges and universities in the region. It is worth noting, however, that TU's tuition is actually low given the average rates of private colleges and universities in Georgia and around the nation. This is by design as price leadership, at least within the independent sector, has long been a strategic priority. TU is also quick to point out the value-added elements of its educational offerings as a way to counter the public school sector's low tuition.

Being small is a strategic advantage and presents many opportunities for TU to shine where the public and larger institution counterparts cannot. TU, like so many other small independents, capitalizes on the strategic advantage of being small... and nimble. Few would argue, including the proponents of public higher education, that small independents are not advantaged by their ability to secure and act upon new market opportunities expediently. Those who do not embrace this opportunity typically suffer as we have recently witnessed at Sweetbriar College (Carlson, 2015; Kolowich, 2015). As many as 250 other schools could experience the same fate as Sweetbriar, according to one recent estimate (June, 2015).

Organizational Capacity

Many small, independent, colleges and universities are not well endowed. In the independent sector, presidents learn quickly that to be considered well endowed, or capable of weathering sustained periods of financial stress, requires a much more significant bank account than most realize. One might be tempted to think that $20 million is a great deal of funds to support an institution. It is not when your annual draw on endowments is probably averaging 4%.

TU is tuition-driven, which translates into enrollment periods three times per academic year with the revenue stream for each being essential to fund the operating budget.

Perhaps more importantly, the absence of a large endowment has served to sharpen the skills of presidents of small independents to generate the level of revenue to not only sustain the school but also grow it. TU's story is certainly a case in point. The question of managing capacity with such tight operating margins goes without saying. Keeping in mind that all credible small, independent, schools such as TU have to meet the same quality standards as their competition who are regionally accredited, it is carried out with extraordinary efficiencies. In fact, thriving small colleges and universities are often models for operational efficiency.

Monitoring and Measuring Progress

In order to assure that the school is moving in the right direction, at all of the operating levels of TU, a unique document labeled the *Strategic Operational Priorities* report was created, which illustrates the specific operational goal to be carried out within a 12- to 18-month period, within the divisions and departments; the individual most responsible for seeing completion of that priority; additional personnel involved in the effort; timeline for completion; and current status. This document is aligned to the overarching institutional goals reported in the *Plan for Strategic Action*, which is in its third iteration since 2006. That document is further aligned back to the stated goals that are shared with major constituencies, including TU accreditors. This alignment is also central to TU's success as the overarching institutional goals feed the strategic operational priorities, and action taken at the division and department levels (see Figure 4.1).

For all strategic operational priorities, a single member of the Administrative Team is always identified as the key owner of individual items, to include the President and all Vice Presidents. This ownership is designed to assure that all purported priorities are monitored and carried out with the highest level of attention. This also assures that accountability for carrying out these priorities is transparent. At least once per month over the 12- to 18-month period of time, each member of the Administrative Team, including the President, is required to report to the entire group on his or her progress staying the course to meet the priority deadline.

Figure 4.1 Thomas University Strategic Process

Redirecting Priorities

One of the most appealing attributes of this strategic model is the ability to redirect priorities rather than continue to expend resources on initiatives that no longer serve to support those overarching institutional goals. This is not to suggest that the overall strategy should be subject to risky and too frequent redirection. In fact, at TU the overarching strategic direction has changed little since 2006. What has changed is the addition of promising initiatives as opportunities presented themselves and a vastly improved operational enterprise that carries it all out.

When redirecting priorities has occurred, it was typically due to a newly discovered awareness that the yield expected from a particular initiative was not really materializing, or a more rewarding direction was discovered. When this occurs, the principal A Team member most responsible for that particular initiative brings their view back to the entire leadership group. It is their responsibility to show others on the team why an effort must be redirected. This level of ownership is critical to the successful application of TU's strategy model.

The Model in Practice

Embracing a more fluid approach to long- and short-term strategy formulation has guided major decisions and actions at TU. Specific work in the PRC is an example of how the approach has been instrumental in achieving a breakthrough strategy.

As of this writing TU has over 1,200 students enrolled in a specially designed, in-country, delivery of 1 year of academic study in the fields of business and nursing. It is expected to grow much larger. Few schools in the world can claim this level of activity in the PRC and none can within the educational field of nursing. TU's current President had a similar successful PRC-based program at his last small, independent, college where he held the position of Provost.

Many educational institutions and even more businesses have tried and failed in the PRC. Those failures can typically be attributed to several overarching missteps in analyzing the opportunities in the PRC and structuring operations to act on them. The missteps include:

- Underestimating the degree to which cultural differences would influence outcomes
- Taking on more risk than the organization can withstand
- Not accepting the fact that most successful ventures require a considerable amount of time to come to fruition...patience is an absolute
- Perhaps most damaging to a college or university...not engaging key constituencies in the formulation of an international strategy and execution of programs

TU's approach to this breakthrough opportunity called for and was undertaken with the following:

- Entering into exploratory engagement with PRC partners with a healthy dose of caution yet recognizing that even the smallest piece of such a huge market could yield great returns for the institution; this met the initial test of a breakthrough opportunity
- Initially treating the development of this program area as an auxiliary enterprise and not becoming operationally dependent upon it until everything was running and producing at the level of expectation to make it a mainstream initiative; it is now part of the core

- Incrementally building the operational support system (to include people and processes) to manage this initiative and not overinvesting in the costs to do so
- Continuous assessment of the return on investment, particularly as the initiative grew and increasing demands were placed on the institution
- Perhaps most important and certainly a central element of this strategy approach, making timely decisions, to include commitments on behalf of the institution during critical negotiations at the onset of partnerships

In Summary

In spite of the significant challenges that higher education has had to face over the past decade, Thomas University stands as an example of a small, independent university that has managed not only to survive but also to thrive. In looking back over this time period, it is apparent that not much was left to chance. Decision making, resource allocation, structuring of people, and processes have all been carried out with overarching strategic goals identified, shared, and converted into real operational actions. The *Plan for Strategic Action* at TU has been employed to keep all major constituencies, and particularly those with influence on the outcomes, focused.

References

Association of Private Sector Colleges and Universities. (2015). *2015 Fact Sheet*. [2015 Fact Sheet].

Astin, A.W., & Lee, B.T. (1974). *The Invisible Colleges*. New York, NY: McGraw Hill.

Beard, D.F. (2009, May/June). Successful applications of the balanced scorecard in higher education. *Journal of Education for Business, 84*(5), 83.

Bonvillian, G., & Murphy, R. (1996). *The Liberal Arts College Adapting to Change: The Survival of Small Schools*. New York, NY: Garland Publishing.

Boyer, E. (1987). *College: The Undergraduate Experience in America.* New York, NY: Harper & Row.

Breneman, D. (1994). *Liberal Arts Colleges: Thriving, Surviving, or Endangered?* Washington D.C.: The Brookings Institution.

Carlson, S. (2015, March 13). Sweet Briar's demise is a cautionary tale for other colleges. *The Chronicle of Higher Education, LXI*(26), A6.

Clark, B. (1992). *The Distinctive College.* New Brunswick, NJ: Transaction Publishing.

Council of Independent Colleges. (2014). *The Power of Liberal Arts Education in Independent Colleges.* [Annual Report].

Dooris, M.J. (2004, Fall). Strategic planning in higher education. *New Directions for Institutional Research*, (123), 5–11.

June, A.W. (2015, March 27). How one small college attracted its largest incoming class ever. *The Chronicle of Higher Education, LXI* (28).

Keller, G. (1983). *Academic Strategy: The Management Revolution in Higher Education.*

Kolowich, S. (2015, April 3). The death of a college. *The Chronicle of Higher Education, LXI*(29), A24–A26.

Morrill, R. (Winter 2013). Collaborative strategic leadership and planning in an era of structural change: Highlighting the role of the governing board. *Peer Review, 15*(1), 12–16.

Perez-Pena, R. (March 27, 2014). In a buyer's market, colleges become fluent in the language of business. *The New York Times, A12.*

Roberts, H.V. (Ed.). (1995). *Academic Initiatives in Total Quality for Higher Education.* Milwaukee, WI: ASQC Quality Press.

Seymour, D.T. (1992). *On Q: Causing Quality in Higher Education.* New York, NY: MacMillan Publishing.

Sims, S.J., & Sims, R.R. (1995). *Total Quality Management in Higher Education.* Westport, CT: Praeger Press.

Thelin, J.R. (2011). *A History of American Higher Education.* Baltimore, MD: The Johns Hopkins University Press.

Waldo, W. (2014). *The Seven Steps of Hoshin Planning.* Retrieved from the BMGI Problem Solved Website: https:www.bmgi.com/about.

Ward, D. (July 2013). Sustaining strategic transitions in higher education. *EDUCAUSE Review, 48*(4), 13–22.

CHAPTER 5

Effective Communication to Improve the Quality of University Instruction

Ernesto Schiefelbein F. and Noel F. McGinn

This chapter describes the elements and outcomes of a strategy to transform instructional practices in a midsized, multicampus university in Latin America. A catalytic model approach was used to connect central university management with academic units, mobilize concern about student failure rates, and over time to reach an agreement on a small but significant change in course design. This change prompted further discussion of instructional practices eventually resulting in further changes and improvement of learning outcomes.

The University's Problem

In Chile, as in other countries of Latin America, university enrollments in recent years have increased rapidly so that they now involve a significant proportion of the eligible population. The expansion of access has been greatly welcomed and also has made more evident serious problems of quality and inequality. These challenges have sparked an intense national debate (OECD, 2012).

The population of higher education students in Chile increased almost five times over two decades: from less than 250,000 in 1990 to more than 1.2 million at present. This increase implies that the net enrollment rate of the 18- to 24-year-old population soared from 12% in 1990 to 33% in 2011 (Mineduc, 2012). A prime beneficiary from this expansion has been youth from low income families. In the 1990s, only 25% of students in higher education came from families in the lower three-fifths of the income distribution. At present they constitute 40% of the total enrollment.

Students enter university with different levels of preparedness, linked to the secondary school they attended. Students in Chile attend one of three kinds of secondary schools: free municipal, subsidized private, or fee-charging private. Average scores on a national achievement test for students attending free schools are about one standard deviation below those of students attending fee-charging private schools (Mineduc, 2011). Most students in the lower three-fifths of the income distribution attend municipal schools, whereas most of those in the higher quintiles attend fee-charging schools.

Differences in achievement test scores are as a consequence attributable in part to differences in the quality of the secondary school attended. In Chile, teacher attendance rates are lowest in free and subsidized schools, as is actual time spent by the teacher in the classroom, compared with that of teachers in fee-charging schools. As a consequence, teachers in the free and subsidized schools cover less of the official curriculum on which the national achievement test is based (Arango, 2008). Estimates are that students in schools in lower income neighborhoods are taught about 50% of the official curriculum (Centro de Estudios, 2013).

Students' levels of academic preparation are also influenced by methods of teaching. The predominant method of instruction in secondary schools in Chile is teacher-centered, directed at the whole class (frontal teaching), and emphasizes learning by memorization over experimentation or reasoning (Edwards & Calvo, 1995). The results of this ineffective instruction are reflected in reading comprehension: only 20% of the population aged 15–65 years has achieved a level of functional literacy sufficient to meet the demands of daily life and work in a complex and advanced society (IALS-OECD, 2000).

In effect, therefore, more than half of the current students entering higher education in Chile have difficulties in understanding what they read, a fundamental skill required for success in the university. In addition, as an increasing proportion of students represent the "first generation" of their families to attain this level of education, more students than in previous years have little understanding of the demands of the culture of the university (Larraín & Zurita, 2008). Taken together, these factors help explain why only half of the students who enter the university actually complete the requirements for graduation (Elacqua, 2012).

Student failure of courses and consequent failure to graduate was of great concern to the university, which is the subject of this chapter. Created in 1989, it was founded with a mission to enable children from lower income families to complete higher education. The university actively pursued recruitment of first-generation students. By 2011, total enrollment had grown to 20,000, distributed across 4 campuses and 30 programs. Two-thirds of the students in the university come from low-income families, attend secondary schools in lower income neighborhoods, and finance their university studies with loans.

In pursuit of its mission, the university seeks to prepare students who will play an important role in Chilean society. It offers a full range of professional career programs (e.g., medicine, psychology, industrial engineering), each of which grants a professional degree on completion. As in other universities in Chile, all students in a given program take the same fixed set of courses.

Although many of the university's students are first generation, its professors are not. Most were raised in middle and upper income families and studied in secondary schools located in higher income neighborhoods. Generalizing from their personal experience, these professors expected that entering students would have the basic skills and knowledge necessary to master the curriculum in their field. They had no idea that many of the terms used in their lectures went completely "over the heads" of many students. A simple example: in mathematics students could grasp the meaning of a vernacular term such as "casual," but miss the significance of more technically precise terms such as "fortuitous," "chance," or "random."

The difference in social origins of students and professors poses a basic dilemma for the university. If it continues with current method of frontal teaching and high standards, students from lower quality schools will continue to be likely to fail to graduate and the university will perpetuate the social gap (which is a root cause of the students' failure). If professors lower their standards to take into account low levels of prior knowledge, this will limit learning of the existing curriculum and produce graduates whose skills and knowledge are insufficient to compete in the labor market, again perpetuating the social gap.

In order to address this issue, the university first had to learn what was being taught in the various programs. Most professors were teaching without a detailed course description or syllabus (often providing only a list of recommended readings). In addition, most of the courses in the university are taught by part-time professors who also teach in other universities. In the absence of a syllabus, the university had no way to insure that what was being taught in one course was compatible with that taught in other courses in a given program.

Prior to this, the university had made several efforts to overcome the gap between prior knowledge and demands of the programs. The Governing Board of the university increased the proportion of professors with postgraduate degrees, encouraged professors to assess their own teaching, and sought advice from leaders of other universities that had been successful in their efforts to raise the quality of teaching. It also sought to improve the integration of first-generation students into the university culture. These actions had little effect on overall completion rates, however. As a consequence, in 2006 the Board created a working group to measure and explain more fully the problem of failure and non-completion, to establish priorities, and to identify possible strategies of solution.

Analysis of Paths to Solution

The success of students in higher education is explained in part by factors that are essentially unchangeable, such as experiences in early childhood. Students are, however, to a certain degree malleable. Actions taken, once a student is attending the university can improve academic performance. It is possible once students are enrolled to reduce gaps in student knowledge and to improve their study habits, to raise their reading ability and improve their use of time and in general increase their capacity to relate concepts and learn more. For example, through interventions that help students achieve academic successes, it is possible to build a positive feedback loop linking their sense of self-efficacy (in academic endeavors) with self-esteem resulting in greater effort (Bresó,

2011; Chan, 2008; Feria, 2010). Taking limitations of prior knowledge and learning ability into account, it is possible to employ incentives that increase the probability of academic success and eventual graduation.

On the other hand, few remedial programs have had success in Chilean higher education. Nor, have they had striking success in American universities (Bettinger & Long, 2009; Complete College America, 2012). Even though college students in the United States can maintain a regular course load by taking up to 40% of their courses as remedial without grades (NCSL, 2012; Peter D. Hart Research Associates, 2005), graduation rates fall well below expectations. In Chile, because all students in a given program take the same fixed set of courses those who fail a course must repeat it in the following semester along with the regular load. This separation of students from their cohort reduces the likelihood of eventual completion (Cornelius-White, 2007).

The remedial courses that are more often successful are those that involve students as active participants in the teaching–learning process. This can be achieved by asking students to prepare themselves before class, usually by appropriate reading, reflection on questions based on the material, or doing exercises or carrying out applications, followed up by discussion in class. These apparently simple actions have various positive effects on the teaching and learning process. The mental responses they engender include increased familiarity with the terminology (vocabulary) used by the professor; formulation of questions to clarify doubts and misunderstandings of the material; increased confidence in ability to participate in class (which facilitates the professor's task); and increased self-esteem resulting in greater effort (Coulter & Smith, 2012; Herreid & Schiller, 2013; Koontz & Plank, 2011).

The university's review of research found programs in several other universities that had succeeded in promoting active student participation in the teaching–learning process with consequent reduction in course failure rates. The review indicated that it is possible to get students to prepare their classes but that some effort is required, and that the use of adequate incentives requires commitment of professors and strong leadership by the administration. It did not seem that required methods and structures would work in all instances (Duranczyk et al., 2004; Wilcox & Angelis, 2011). An effort was made to understand the conditions in which this strategy would be effective with first-generation university students in Chile.

Near the end of 2011, two unexpected events galvanized the university into action. The first was a visit by university officials to two universities in Germany that recently had improved their completion rate. The experience of these universities demonstrated that, in order to improve academic performance, students had to spend more time on study, and that this requires overcoming the tradition of review of what the professor covered in the previous class. Second, a visit to the university by a professor from Harvard University introduced officials to the use of the "flipped class" method (Berrett, 2012; Mazur, 2012) to teach science. This professor also recommended getting students to read in advance about what would be covered in their next class. Given this background, the Governing Board in September 2011 approved the introduction of a method of Reading for Active Participation (RAP) at the beginning of the 2012 academic year. Immediately afterwards, 150 program directors and professors participated in a workshop operated as a "flipped class."

In introducing RAP, officials expected that it would be relatively easy to get students to read a brief text before each class. A more serious challenge was how to prepare appropriate texts for the 5,000 new students who would begin classes in 30 different programs in March 2012. This would require describing the specific content of each weekly class session and its accompanying reading. These outlines or syllabuses would include some 60–70 pages for each of 156 distinct courses. The courses are distributed across four campuses and involve 800 sections. It was a large endeavor, but university officials were hopeful that given several experiments in previous years, and the outcome of the September 2011 workshop, that the innovation could be implemented successfully.

Designing a New Model for Teaching, Communicating, and Implementing

The challenge facing new (first-generation) students was highlighted by a diagnostic study of "study methods and habits" carried out by the Department of Undergraduate Teaching in March 2012. The study showed that 64% of the new students needed to improve their study habits and methods, and that 40% lacked adequate physical space for studying (Unpublished).

The working group decided to provide students with a maximum of two pages (1,000 words) of reading for each class included in the syllabus. The reading could be completed in 5–7 minutes (in many cases en route to the University from home or during a break). While the syllabus would describe the course themes and learning objectives, the anticipatory text would define for each session the specialized terms to be used, and introduce the critical knowledge required to understand the session. This would compensate for gaps in knowledge of students from those secondary schools that did not provide complete curriculum coverage.

The Department of Undergraduate Teaching and the program directors oversaw the preparation of the syllabus (course outline) and anticipatory reading material for each of the 156 courses given in the first semester of each program. Each syllabus was authored by a professor chosen from the regular faculty. The authors in turn coordinated their efforts with the professors who would teach one or more of the sections of the courses. Authors were compensated for their time once the syllabus was approved by the other professors offering the course.

Students learned about RAP when they first contacted the university to ask about programs and requirements for admission. They were informed again on enrollment, and during the orientation sessions in the first week of classes. On these occasions, students were told about how doing the preparatory reading would benefit them. They also learned how to access the syllabuses and anticipatory readings on SAGAF, the computer platform provided by the university.

The justification of the RAP method to professors was simple and direct—"when students read, they usually participate more actively in class and understand the answers professors give to their questions"—emphasizing that this benefit comes only if students actually do the reading at least once. In effect, students learn more when they accept (some measure of) responsibility for their own learning. To motivate students to read, research had shown, professors should begin each class with a question based on the anticipatory reading directed at a few students chosen at random, and followed by assignment of a grade based on the response given (Dunlap, 2012; Leamnson, 1999; Nilson, 2010; Weimer, 2011).

The introduction of RAP asked the professors to make six changes in their teaching. They were asked to:

1. cover, in each class, the topic scheduled in the syllabus and anticipatory reading (because otherwise the students' reading would serve no purpose reducing their likelihood of preparing for the class);
2. dedicate the first 4 min of each session to asking one to three students chosen randomly to comment on a question based on the anticipatory text;
3. evaluate out loud the students' response assigning a grade (that would contribute a small amount to the final grade);
4. follow by asking students for any doubts raised by the reading and providing clarification;
5. carry out the rest of the session in the usual manner (with no further reference to the students' anticipatory reading); and
6. at the end of the class recommend that students download material for the next session from SAGAF to determine whether it raised any questions that the professor should answer at the next session.

While these changes seemed simple enough, previous pilot tests had revealed that some professors neglected to ask one or more students about the reading, and some neglected to evaluate the response. Some professors appeared to resist assigning a grade to motivate students to read. They agreed that reading is a habit acquired in early childhood in the family and that some students lacking that experience needed to learn its benefits for university study, but felt uncomfortable assigning a grade to the students' response (even though the assigned grade had only a small impact on the final grade).

University officials anticipated, therefore, that the 700 professors would vary in their implementation of the six-part innovation. How would it be possible to determine the extent to which RAP was being put into practice and to persuade professors to implement the program as designed? Draconian regulations, classroom observation, and incentives or sanctions for compliance were ruled out.

A Catalytic Model to Change Instructional Practices Without Direct Intervention

The initial steps taken were intended to create conditions that over time will stimulate and facilitate changes in the behavior of both students and their professors. The interventions taken, while worthwhile, were not ends in themselves but instead intended as a catalyst for change (Christensen et al., 2006; Waddock & Post, 1991). Student study practices were deemed easier to change than professors' instructional practices, but changes in the former (combined with other actions) would contribute to changes in the latter.

An effort was made to encourage family members to persuade students to adopt the practices of the RAP method. In January and February, at the time of enrollment, the Admissions Office introduced new students (and family members who accompanied them) to the syllabus and RAP, demonstrating how to use the information system to access the material for each class in every one of their first semester courses. Emphasis was placed on the importance of preparing for upcoming classes by reading the anticipatory texts.

Student response to the introduction of RAP was assessed by voluntary (anonymous) surveys of students distributed and returned using the university's computerized information system. The first survey, in March 2012, was designed to detect startup problems students had with the method (e.g., access to anticipatory texts), and the extent to which professors and they were following the method. Discussion groups were held with professors on each campus to identify their perception of benefits and problems generated by the innovation, to elicit suggestions for improvements in the design for the second semester (August to December 2012), and to plan changes in the syllabuses and anticipatory texts prior to the first semester of 2013.

Surveys carried out at the end of the first and second semester assessed the implementation of the RAP method. This implementation involved seven different elements (e.g., explanation of the purpose of the method, access to material on SAGAF, training of professors in use of the method, etc.). As Table 5.1 indicates, student approval increased directly with the number of elements of the method that they experienced. At the end of the first semester, the "grade" students assigned to RAP (a measure of approval) increased directly with the number of elements implemented. The survey at the end of the second semester indicated that student reading of the anticipatory text increased directly with the number of elements carried out.

Implementation of the method improved significantly in each of the next 2 years. Table 5.2 reports on three elements that characterize the rate of improvement. Over the 3 years the proportion of professors asking questions about reading of the anticipatory text increased from 15.9% to 92.3%, and the proportion assigning grades increased from 7.6% in 2012 to 84.6% in 2014. During this period the deans and the program directors used the survey results to tell professors about student enthusiasm for the method and their increased reading of course material. Sessions held with professors on each campus discussed their experiences with the introduction of the method. The next step was to show that student enthusiasm for the Method reflected their awareness of improved learning (and higher course grades).

Table 5.1 Level of Implementation, Student Evaluation of RAP, and Reading of Text (2012)

Elements Implemented	Survey July 2012		Survey November 2012	
	Grade Assigned to MRP*	Number of Cases	Always Reads Text	Number of Cases
None	2.7	71	0	51
One	2.9	137	0	9
Two	3.7	176	15.2%	33
Three	4.3	165	25.5%	47
Four	4.7	153	50.5%	107
Five	5.4	90	85.5%	131
Six	5.1	48	100.0%	131
Seven	5.5	30	~	~
Total	2.88	870	61.7%	509

*In response to the question "What grade would you give to RAP?," students assigned values ranging from 0 to 7. In Chile a passing grade is 4 or above.

Table 5.2 Opinion of Students About Classroom Implementation of RAP 2012–2014

Implementation Elements	July 2012	July 2013	July 2014
Do you know why the RAP method has been introduced?			
(Yes)	67.2%	86.1%	
One or more professor asks a question about the	15.9%	72.4%	92.3%

reading at the beginning of the class			
(If a question is asked) the response to the question is assigned a grade	7.6%	55.5%	84.6%
Number of cases	870	1473	1026

Impact of Student Reading Before Class on Academic Performance (Grades and Course Completion)

Grades are dependent on several factors. Difficulty level varies from course to course and across disciplines and programs as well as from professor to professor. The importance attributed to performance on the final examination varies across courses. Some professors take into account student participation in class in assigning grades, whereas others do not. Grades can also vary as a function of university norms (e.g., grade inflation reflects a general relaxation of common standards). Grade point averages reflect all these factors. Even so, we can expect that students whose prior (course relevant) knowledge is high will do better than those whose knowledge is low. This is one reason why university grades are correlated with admission test scores and secondary school grade point averages.

The impact of prior knowledge is minimized by comparing changes in grade point averages over time. Students with low prior knowledge should be able to increase their knowledge as much (if not more) than those who start with high levels of knowledge. To observe the impact of reading the anticipatory text on learning (as measured by grades), we compared average grades across courses for each of the three succesive semesters. As we are comparing grades for the same individuals at three points time, constant factors (such as family income and education, admission test scores, and academic program) should not explain any differences that appear.

Table 5.3 presents the average grade point averages according to whether the student reports reading the anticipatory text. At the end of the first semester, students who said they read the text had an average grade point average of 4.80, while those who said they did not read it had an average of 4.71. This difference is not statistically significant. The difference in grade point averages is larger at the end of the second semester of enrollment (Spring 2012) but still not statistically significant. By the end of the third semester, however, the difference is large enough to be considered reliable. Students who say they read the anticipatory text have higher grade point averages than their classmates who do not read.

Table 5.3 *Grades and Courses Passed by "Readers" and "Non-readers" Who First Enrolled in March 2012*

Student Usually Reads the Anticipatory Text	First Semester (Fall) 2012			Second Semester (Spring) 2012			Third Semester (Fall) 2013		
	GPA	% Courses Passed	N	GPA	% Courses Passed	N	GPA	% Courses Passed	N
YES	4.80	88.5%	298	4.72	85.9%	293	4.82	39.4%	275
NO	4.71	86.9%	139	4.58	81.1%	138	4.63	33.9%	127
Level of significance*	0.30	0.42		0.15	0.06		0.03	0.01	
Number of students**			437			431			402

*Probability of the difference between the two GPAs could be obtained by chance. The smaller the number, the more likely that the difference is not by chance (but instead is a result of having read the anticipatory text).

**Some 7.7% (23) of the reading group drop out, or are repeating a year while 8.6% (12) of the non-reading group have dropped out or are repeating.

A similar result is obtained by comparing the proportion of courses passed. The difference is insignificant at the end of the first semester, but by the end of the third semester, reading students pass more courses than those who do not read. Students who fail courses in Chile are obliged to repeat them, and students who repeat courses are more likely to end up leaving the university before graduation. Course failure is not the only reason for deserting, but a comparison of the number of students in the cohort of 437 who answered the survey in the first semester of 2012 with those still enrolled in the second and third semesters suggests that 7.7% of the read-before-class group dropped out by the end of the third semester, whereas 8.6% of the non-reading group dropped out. If the effect of reading before class is cumulative over time, by the end of the 8th or 10th semester of study, the two groups of students will be markedly different in their academic performance and degree completion.

The effect of the RAP method should increase over time as more and more professors implement all of its elements, and as more students understand the benefits of reading before class and learn to study effectively. A less tangible but important impact of RAP is changes in what occurs in the classroom. Implementation of the method required small changes in professors' conduct of their classes. These changes set in motion other changes that may over time have a more profound impact. In various panel discussions, students reported that as a consequence of the anticpatory reading they felt more confident in class. This confidence led to asking questions during the professor's lecture, which in some courses resulted in active discussions. In separate meetings, professors reported that student participation in class had increased; they felt this was a positive outcome, that students were now more interested in what the professor was teaching.

If the effects of RAP are in fact cumulative and the method continues to improve the quality of instruction in the University, this case can serve as an example for other institutions seeking to overcome educational inequalities by providing first-generation students with a more effective teaching program.

References

Arango, A. (2008, July 30). *The failings of Chile's educational system: Institutionalized inequality and a preference for the affluent.* Retrieved

February 13, 2013, from Council on Hemispheric Affairs: http://www.coha.org/the-failings-of-chile%E2%80%99s-education-system-institutionalized-inequality-and-a-preference-for-the-affluent/

Berrett, D. (2012). How 'flipping' the classroom can improve the traditional lecture. *The Chronicle of Higher Education*, *58* (25), A16–A18.

Bettinger, E.P., & Long, B.T. (2009). Addressing the needs of underprepared students in higher education: Does college remediation work? *Journal of Human Resources (http://www.nber.org/papers/w11325)*, *44* (3).

Bresó, E.S. (2011). Can a self-efficacy-based intervention decrease burnout, increase engagement, and enhance performance? A quasi-experimental study. *Higher Education, 61*(4), 339–355.

Centro de Estudios. (2013). *Implementación del currículum de Educación Media en Chile.Serie Evidencias.* Santiago, Chile: Ministerio de Educación.

Chan, J.C.-F. (2008). Effects of different evaluative feedback on student's self-efficacy in learning. *Instructional Science, 38*(1), 37–58.

Christensen, C.M., Baumann, H., Ruggles, R., & Sadtler, T.M. (2006). Disruptive innovation for social change. *Harvard Business Review, 84*(12), 94–101.

Complete College America. (2012). *Remediation: Higher Education's Bridge to Nowhere.* Washington DC: Complete College America.

Cornelius-White, J. (2007). Learner-centered teacher-student relationships are effective: A meta-analysis. *Review of Educational Research, 77*(1), 113–143.

Coulter, C.J., & Smith, S. (2012). The impact of preclass reading assignments on class performance. *Currents in Pharmacy Teaching and Learnng, 4*(2), 109–112.

Dunlap, J. (2012). *Encouraging Students to Read Before Class.* Denver, CO: Center for Faculty Development, University of Colorado.

Duranczyk, I.M., Higbee, J.L., & Lundell, D.B. (2004). *Best Practices for Access and Retention in Higher Education.* Minneapolis MN: Center for Research on Developmental Education and Urban Literacy, Urban College, University of Minnesota.

Edwards, V., & Calvo, C. (1995). *El liceo por dentro, estudio etnográfico sobre prácticas de trabajo en educación media.* Santiago, Chile: Ministerio de Educación, Programa MECE.

Elacqua, G. (2012). Education: Chile's students demand reform. *Americas Quarterly, Winter.*

Feria, J.V. (2010). Judgments of self-perceived academic competence and their differential impact on students' achievement motivation, learning approach and academic performance. *European Journal for the Psychology of Education, 25*(4), 519–536.

Herreid, C.F., & Schiller, N.A. (2013). Case studies and the flipped classroom. *Journal of College Science Teaching, 42*(5), 62–65.

IALS-OECD. (2000). *Literacy in the Information Age. Final Report of the International Adult Literacy Survey.* Ottawa: OECD, Statistics Canada.

Koontz, T.M., & Plank, K.M. (2011). Can reading questions foster active learning? A study of six college courses. *Journal on Excellence in College Teaching, 22*(3), 23–46.

Larraín, C., & Zurita, S. (2008). The new student loan system in Chile's higher education. *Higher Education, 55*(6), 683–702.

Leamnson, R. (1999). *Thinking about Teaching and Learning: Developing Habits of Learning with First Year College and University Students.* Baltimore, MD: Stylus Publishing.

Mazur, E. (2012). Farewell, lecture? *Science, 323*(5910), 50–51.

Mineduc. (2012). *Análisis y Recomendaciones para el Sistema de Financiamiento Estudiantil.* Santiago, Chile: Ministerio de Educación y Cultura, Comisión de Financiamiento Estudiantil.

Mineduc. (2011). *Resultados Nacionales SIMCE 2010.* Santiago, Chile: Ministerio de Educación y Cultura, SIMCE.

NCSL. (2012). *Hot Topics in Higher Education: Reforming Remedial Education.* Washington, DC, http://www.ncsl.org/research/education/improving-college-completion-reforming-remedial.aspx: National Conference of State Legislatures.

Nilson, L.B. (2010). Getting students to do the readings. In L.B. Nilson, *Teaching At Its Best: A Research-Based Resource for College Instructors (3rd Edition)* (pp. 211–222). San Francisco: Jossey-Bass.

OECD. (2012). *Quality Assurance in Higher Education in Chile: Reviews of National Policies for Education.* Paris: OECD, http://www.oecd.org/chile/Quality%20Assurance%20in%20Higher%20Education%20in%20Chile%20-%20Reviews%20of%20National%20Policies%20for%20Education.pdf.

Peter D. Hart Research Associates. (2005). *Rising to the Challenge: Are High School Graduates Prepared for College and Work?* Washington, DC: Achieve.

Waddock, S.A., & Post, J.E. (1991). Social entrepreneurs and catalytic change. *Public Administration Review, 51*(5), 393–401.

Weimer, M. (2011). A comparison of two strategies for getting students to do the reading. *The Teaching Professor, 25*(1), 4.

Wilcox, K.C., & Angelis, J.L. (2011). *Best Practices from High-Performing High Schools: How Successful Schools Help Students Stay in School and Thrive.* New York: Teachers College Press.

CHAPTER 6

Going Online: Pitfalls and Best Practices in Distance Education

Mac Powell

Declining enrollments and the expanding universe of students made possible by technology all over the world have made conversations about the use of distance education unavoidable in higher education. Administrators are asked by their Boards how technology is being implemented to expand the reach of their universities, and faculty often watch on in horror as the traditional classroom lecture format is declining in favor compared to "flipped classrooms," competency-based learning, asynchronous online lectures, adaptive learning, and virtual advising. Between 2002 and 2012, "the number of undergraduate students taking online courses increased by approximately 23 percent" (Braude & Merrill, 2013) and as online courses have grown more and more common place, Parker et al. (2011) estimate that 61% of liberal arts colleges, 79% of research universities, and 82% of community college offer some online options. This chapter looks at the history and current development of distance education and provides administrators and faculty guidance and best practices on the many decisions required to successfully implement technology to expand academic offerings.

The Rise of Distance Education

Distance education is hardly a new phenomenon in higher education. The practice dates back as far as the 1800, and was common in the United States through correspondence schools in the 1900s that offered rural and poor learners the opportunity to expand their skills, often in the disciplines of business, history, accounting, and administrative services (Harting & Erthal, 2005). As education in the United States grew with the return of veterans from World War II and the passage of the Higher Education Act, the number of institutions and types of programs to serve them swelled (Geiger, 2014). The adaptation of education to serve different segments of the population (veterans, women, working adults, and other nontraditional students) led administrators around the country to continue to ask questions about how to expand access and provide more convenient pathways to educational institutions. And, while adaptation occurred with night courses, part-time programs, and instructional sequencing to ease pathways to degrees, nothing was more transformative to education than the almost overnight ubiquity of networked computers and the realization that knowledge was no longer bound to lecture halls and library stacks. Early adopters, like Glen R. Jones at Jones International University and John Sperling, who created the University of Phoenix through the Institute for Professional Development's partnership with the University of San Francisco, saw the opportunity of taking the classroom to the masses through technology (Breneman et al., 2006; Harting & Erthal, 2005). These efforts, however, were only the early tremors in the seismic shift of private profits and not-for-profits into online education to serve a growing population of adult learners returning to school. What distance learning was, is, and could be is a product of the mass availability and mass comfort with technology balanced against the traditions of education, which yield slowly to the inevitability of evolution.

This evolution of distance education that began mainly as correspondence classes, where students would be sent workbooks or textbooks by mail and asked to complete exercises, which would be returned to the correspondent school, graded, and a certificate of completion created transformed with the creation of the Internet. The Internet initially eliminated only the mailing of documents, as schools such as Fielding Graduate School in Santa Barbra, California and others now had the ability to communicate and transmit materials (mostly text-based content rather than audio or visual materials) instantaneously. Several technology firms saw the opportunity to create warehouses of documents (such as written lectures, assignments, readings, and examinations) and the ability to create discussion boards for students to interact in real time (synchronous) and at their own pace (asynchronous). Many universities used online platforms as augmentations to their traditional courses, posting assignments and readings that might traditionally be held on reserve in the university's library collections. The platforms expanded to give faculty the ability to have students submit assignments to the platform (or electronic dropbox), grade and repost the assignments in the platform, and keep a constantly available and updated gradebook for students. The richness of content evolved as the technology and bandwidth expanded, and professors were soon given the ability to transmit and record lectures (first in audio and later with video) giving students the ability to participate in real time or to watch them at their own pace and from any location. As can be imagined, any resistance to technology in the classroom was magnified a hundred-fold with the growing possibility that academic content (and the lecture itself) could be recorded and owned by the university, perhaps thereby making the faculty less important, if not obsolete. The fears of faculty have largely not come to pass, but faculty remain the heart and soul of most institutions, and adopting, expanding, and excelling at distance education requires an understanding of its strengths and limitations and an administration that is able to partner with faculty. These challenges will be addressed later, but as a concluding note on "traditional" online courses, it is important to understand what distance education looks like for students as of this writing. Most students arrive at a course through a web-portal and are immediately met by an experience that is wholly two-dimensional. Many universities work with vendors that can help build more "robust environments," but few as of today are able to provide much more than inspiring images, text, and perhaps a welcome video. There are chat boxes and classroom updates (again, almost all in text form), and there is navigation that typically takes students through learning units (which are essentially a file folder with elements such as readings, quizzes, videos, lectures, and simulations). Most students that take online courses today have little interaction with the faculty outside of discussion boards and limited feedback on assignments. Institutions generally shy away from synchronous lectures or activities (where students arrive in the online environment all at once and participate remotely) because in most cases students are from diverse geographic regions of the country (sometimes even diverse countries) or have outside commitments that make being in one place at a particular time inconvenient or impossible. I have taught several classes where my students logged in from military combat overseas, or from an aircraft carrier across the world, and enforcing their attendance in a 6 p.m. Pacific Standard Time lecture was not feasible.

These current practices in online technology are in some ways accompanied by a movement that gained notoriety in the early 2000s when some of the very best courses offered by elite universities like Harvard, Stanford, Princeton, and Penn were offered online for free. Massive Open Online Courses (MOOC) and the MOOC movement faded initially for mostly economic reasons, which will be discussed later, but the MOOC signaled a shift in how people began to think about distance education. Why would every university offer a Political Science 101 course if the best political scientist in the world was willing to give away his lectures and learning materials for free? The technology platforms quickly adapted to the opportunity and created adaptive learning opportunities, where the course content and assessments shift according to the abilities and learning style of the learner. The kernel of the MOOC is that hundreds of thousands of people from around the world can take a course together, synchronously or asynchronously, from the best instructors in the world (often for free), and the technology around the courses put student learning at the heart of the exercise.

As a significant early adopter of technology and with a focus on innovation and access, Western Governors University grew to become a significant player in what has become known as competency-based learning. Though existing in many forms, the basic premise is that learners can access prerecorded content online and complete assignments that demonstrate that they have mastered the recorded content that matches to learning outcomes in an academic program. Apart from giving learners the opportunity to self-pace, competency-based learning did something even more significant, redefined the meaning of the "credit hour," or the seat time that a student had to occupy in order to qualify for academic credit (and the financial aid dollars precisely measured against that credit paid to the institution). This decoupling of seat time and student learning signal a fundamental shift in how academics think about what constitutes appropriate rigor and student contact, and requires administrators to be even more familiar with accreditation standards, assessment, and the complexities of financial aid and other forms of student funding.

With over a century of distance education and three decades of online education, more than three quarters of the nation's colleges and universities now offer some form of online course; about one-in-four college graduates have taken at least one course online; and "among college graduates who have taken a class online, 15% have earned a degree entirely online" (Parker et al., 2011, p. 3, 7). This explosion has given rise to a number of questions about the effectiveness and quality of online education, its true value as a mode of academic delivery, its ability to lower the cost of education, what constitutes best practices, and the appropriate role of faculty and administrators in this evolution of what constitutes higher education.

Educational Effectiveness and Quality: Does Online Education Work?

Administrators and faculty are often asked about the quality of online offerings, and a significant amount of skepticism exists as to the quality of an online degree versus a traditional degree. Young adults are just as skeptical about online education as older adults; "just three-in-ten American adults (29%) say a course taken online provides an equal educational value to one taken in a classroom"; by contrast, "fully half of college presidents (51%) say online courses provide the same value" (Parker et al., 2011, p. 3). In another study, Parker et al. (2011, p. 11) found that only 29% of all respondents said online classes offer an equal value to on-site courses. Studies on the value "signaled" by a degree from an online University point out that the skepticism is shared by employers, calling into question for many the value proposition of the online degree (Parker et al., 2011, p.11). However, while there may be questions at large about the value of online education and a degree offered 100% online, significant research has studied the effectiveness of online course offerings and demonstrated its effectiveness (Scheg, 2015, p. 245). In general, online courses can be just effective or more effective than traditional onsite courses (Bartholomew, 2010; Braude & Merrill, 2013, p. 51; Beck, 2010; Diaz, 2002; Means et al., 2010, p. xiv; Scheg, 2015, pp. 245–246). Research has shown that the effectiveness of the courses is often tied to the discipline and the type of learning that typically occurs, and that "instruction combining online and face-to-face elements had a larger advantage relative to purely face-to-face instruction than did purely online, instruction" (Means et al., 2010, p. xv). For instance, an undergraduate survey course taught in large lecture halls with limited interaction is in many ways comparable to an online course;

materials are presented to a large group of students who digest the material and demonstrate their understanding on an examination. The level of one-on-one engagement may actually be higher in an online course, where attendance is monitored and the faculty engages with the students in regular discussion board posts. Even graduate courses have been shown to be as effective in some disciplines when measuring satisfaction and student learning outcomes (Hansen, 2001, pp. 995–996). Like the characteristics of successful on-site students, successful online students have been found to have characteristics that should be considered when designing and implementing courses; these characteristics include being more disciplined, organized, self-motivated, and technologically knowledgeable" (Hiltz & Goldman, 2004). Structuring courses to attract, retain, and continually engage these students is critical, and often dependent upon the learning management systems (LMS). Learning analytics embedded in some LMS systems can help select at-risk students, which can help administrators redeploy resources, and significantly increase retention, a significant measure for many in determining the success of an online program. However, while there is no substitute for a high-quality faculty member, the best LMS and systems are "...far beyond the capability of individual instructors to create on their own, and are typically developed by teams of cognitive scientist, software engineers, instructional designers, and users interface experts" (Bacow et al., 2012, p. 7).

While there are few agreed-upon standards in modeling what constitutes the very best in online education, a growing number of journals and conferences offer resources to those who seek best practices (Fish and Wickersham, 2009). Alley and Jansak (2001) have identified keys to quality online learning, including creating an environment where knowledge is constructed, not transmitted; where students are provided learning activities that match their learning styles; where courses provide "mental white space" for reflection; where solitary and interpersonal activities are interspersed; where inaccurate learning is identified and corrected; where "Spiral learning" provides for revisiting and expanding prior lessons; and where a master teacher is available to guide the learning process (Alley & Jansak, 2001, pp. 6–17).

Chickering and Ehrmann (1997) contend that the power of online technologies will be fully realized only if their use is consistent with newer pedagogies of teaching that place students more in the role of creators of knowledge. The authors suggest that the best online teaching should encourage contact between students and faculty, develop reciprocity and cooperation among students, use active learning techniques, give prompt feedback, emphasize time on task, communicate high expectations, and respect diverse talents and ways of learning (1997). "High quality online instruction encourages discovery, integration, application, and practices. Instructors need to discover students' learning preferences, integrate technology tools, apply appropriate instructional techniques, put them all into practices, and generate the most suitable method for individuals" (Yang & Cornelious, 2005).

As the research continues to grow, so does the recognition of grant-funded projects to disseminate best practices. Quality Matters, for example, is an organization representing institutions across high education and K-12 that focuses upon peer-reviewed process to certify the quality of an online or blended course. The organization provides rubrics that can help administrators understand the key components of a highly evolved online course and gives administrators and faculty the opportunity to participate in a review process that offers some guidance on whether a university's courses comply with their standards (Quality Matters, 2015). Some of the standards from Quality Matters include learning activities that are tied to learning objectives and program competencies; clear guidance for technical support; utilization of appropriate multimedia and a variety of instructional materials; the course clearly defines the expectations of the students and "netiquette" for online discussions; and that learning activities provide opportunities for interactions that support learning (Quality Matters, 2015).

Given the volume of research and years of practical application, it is clear that high-quality online education is an effective method for delivering high-quality educational content for selected disciplines. The quickly evolving opportunities in educational platforms, a growing number of high-quality content providers, and a quickly expanding locus of scholarship and best practices in online education give faculty and administrators a clearer perspective on the value of online education and a roadmap for quality and educational effectiveness.

The Costs of Implementation and the Cost of Higher Education

The costs of implementing an online educational system can be significant. Many institutions utilize an established Learning Management System, such as Blackboard, most of which would typically charge a per course (or per student per course) fee with certain guaranteed minimums on an annual basis. Additional fees would likely be for technical support for students in the platform and technical support for faculty in the platform, with significantly higher fees for additional built-in content or course design assistance. University administrators currently have build-it versus buy-it options from many vendors who offer universities complete catalogs of courses with built-in textbooks, audio–visual content, examinations, gradebooks, and tracking analytics. These buy-it options often are billed on a per user fee with wireframes and banners adjusted to brand the courses with a particular university's name, color, logos, et cetera. Even more venture capital groups are reaching out to universities to offer online course content, learning management systems, entire degree programs, and recruitment services for a significant portion of tuition revenue (Pianko & Jarrett, 2012). This ever-expanding market is fueled by the $8 billion annual college textbook industry, which sees its role as moving further into content delivery, rather than just content creation (Parker et al., 2011, p. 14).

As schools struggle to achieve enrollment gains and manage debt, more and more are selecting these profit-sharing models rather than purchasing LMS systems, building online colleges, hiring and retaining online faculty, and managing a distinct set of student engagement activities to ensure student success. And, in considering whether to buy-it or build-it, timing should be considered just as seriously as potential costs. Many universities establish launch timelines that are unrealistic given their capabilities, which can ultimately lead to launching poor-quality courses (which will undoubtedly affect student satisfaction and referrals in the long run). Most high-quality online courses take over 100 hours of course design time from an instructor, and then just as many hours of a course designer working with a faculty member to ensure quality and proper student experience. An excellent quality assurance process would have an expert in course design taking the class well before it is seen by students to ensure that content and links function properly. Beyond the frustration of students who experience a poorly designed course, a significant driver of increased costs is poorly functioning course content that cause students and faculty to retain customer service and design services last minute. Some universities have worked with their LMS provider to establish links within each page of a course to identify problems that are sent directly to the faculty or program chair. In a well-constructed system of this kind, all users become quality assurance experts, who provide ongoing feedback to the owner of the course content.

Bacow et al.'s (2012) research into implementation and quality issues across higher education noted administrator's desire to generate revenue, increase international program recognition, and recruit beyond existing geographies to be among the primary drivers of the adoption of online programs. The financial success of added online programming is not guaranteed, with an often intensive initial capital investment, significant competition, and a steep learning curve to successfully deliver the courses. However, the most successful programs were those that "…have established a separate program with a difference (lower) cost structure, often using less expensive space, adjuncts or other lower cost faculty, and a separate administrative apparatus, while charging tuition equal to or even sometimes greater than the tuition charged for traditional courses" (Bacow et al., 2012, p. 9). In analyzing the costs of implementing online education, it is clear that administrators must undergo an extensive review of potential vendors, utilize professional networks and consultant when available to understand current pricing models and vendor options, understand the initial costs and timing of implementation, and grapple with the growing competition and need for quality to preserve the institution's brand and student experience.

The Opportunities of Implementing Distance Education

Most Boards and presidents see online education as an opportunity to expand the geographic reach of their institution and to recruit students that would not traditionally be candidates for their degree programs. Many universities see the added opportunities for purchasing already tested and implemented academic programs as an opportunity to diversify program offerings. While both are possible, a scan of the environment should yield caution. There are many established players in the online marketplace, most of whom have shared administrators and faculty and learned collectively the lessons of online adoption. Challenges with recruitment and retention (Allen & Seaman, 2013; Frankola, 2001; Neumann, 1998) are ominous and often require a rethinking of the role of faculty and advisors. As addressed above, many institutions have adapted to this either by moving almost entirely online or by creating a separate college with distinct differences in the culture and day-to-day work of faculty and staff. In a space with existing competitors, marketing can be a challenge, with an institution's entry not even guaranteeing the potential students who must be cultivated and recruited with different forms of engagement: e-mail, social media videos, online meet-ups, electronic welcome kits, and customer management systems with automated engagement campaigns to monitor a potential student's level of interest prior to admission and registration.

Creating a Culture of Evidence and Excellence in Online Education

The growing opportunities in online education should lead administrators not only to ask whether their institution should adopt online offerings but also to ask how to build cultures of evidence and excellence to differentiate their institutions from peers. According to Twigg (2001) many problems can arise as institutions make the transition to online offerings because of different quality standards and the appropriate measurement of quality and student outcomes in online offerings. Traditional faculty may be resistant not only to teaching online courses but also to recruiting new faculty with specialized expertise, feeling that the shift of focus in pedagogy or specialization might impact their own teaching or departmental importance. These issues transcend just online education, and represent larger discussions about the role of faculty and the "locus of authority" in higher educational institutions as institutions inevitably shift to address changing circumstances (Bowen & Lack, 2013; Bowen & Tobin, 2015). Faculty must remain a central focus of the process of implementing and evaluating program quality, both for as Deubel (2003) has argued, "an instructor's attitude, motivation, and true commitment affect much of the quality of online instruction" (as cited in, Yang & Cornelious, 2005, p. 5).

Obtaining buy-in from faculty and administrators on what qualifies as quality in online development and delivery has been challenging for many institutions because of differences between disciplines. Administrators tend to advocate one-size-fits all templates for course development and archiving, which is often at odds with faculty who desire to have unique versions of their courses. Even finding agreement between faculty and administration on how to evaluate the quality of the teaching, learning, and content in online courses can be difficult. To alleviate some of those tensions, many universities have created online divisions with distinct faculty, administrators, and processes; other universities have created administrative support departments to partner with faculty to design and evaluate courses within the traditional structure of a university. Under any structure, administrators should partner with faculty and staff to recognize best practices within the institution in course design and course delivery. Creating "faculty champions" can help build consensus and buy-in for what constitutes appropriate levels of achievement for both students and faculty. Ultimately, creating excellence and evaluating the quality of courses require a faculty evaluation structure that has the ability to recognize and reward, and subsequently integrate evaluation of online activities into ongoing program review. These evaluations should include both the clarity and relevance of course outcomes, the relevance of course material to the discipline and course outcomes, the quality of participation of faculty and students in online activities, the ease of navigation, the ease of access and integration to course materials, and ongoing evaluation from both the student's and faculty's perspective of the quality of the course design and delivery.

Conclusion

As demand for online courses continue to increase, competition will assuredly continue to push institutions, platforms, and content providers to become more adept. This will come with a need for constant faculty evolution, greater communication and online skills, and greater time commitment to creating a vibrant learning environment in a sea of providers (Gallien & Oomen-Early, 2008, p. 463).

Issues of workload and the evaluation of instructor and design quality will necessarily go hand-in-hand as faculty and administrators work to find a balance between academic freedom, the appropriate role of faculty, workload, and the role of administrators and the Board in shaping the trajectory of an institution trying to adapt to a changing ecology of education. In evaluating whether to make the transition to online education, administrators should keep these balances in mind as they work with faculty to develop programs and courses, carefully consider the costs of implementing online systems, constantly evaluate the quality of outcomes to create competitive advantage and promote value within the institution, and be cognizant of the signaling to external constituents that online education can create and reinforce. Going online is not a simple decision, but rather part of a larger set of strategies aligned with institutional reach and mission (Figure 6.1). Engaging the board, faculty, alumni is critical for buy-in, and empirically evaluating the opportunities and challenges in entering into an increasingly competitive space can help create realistic timelines and budgets to ensure long-term success. In the end, administrators must weigh whether their institution's traditional methods and offerings will continue to hold competitive value in the quickly shifting ecology of higher education or whether they will side with most experts predicting a seismic shift requiring a rethinking of how to expand access, reduce costs, and draw upon the best content from around the globe to capture the attention and imagination of the modern student.

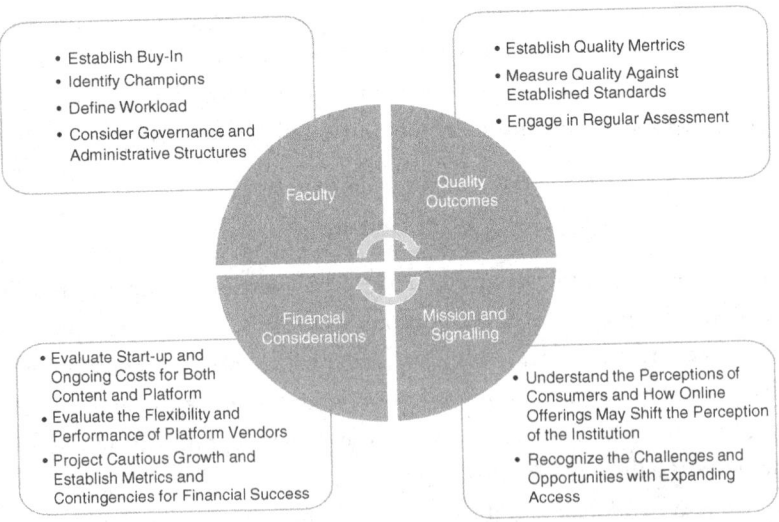

Figure 6.1 Evaluation of the decision to go online.

References

Allen, I.E., & Seaman, J. (2013). *Changing Course: Ten Years of Tracking Online Education in the United States.* Babson Survey Research Group and Quahog Research Group, LLC. Retrieved from http://www.onlinelearningsurvey.com/reports/changingcourse.pdf.

Alley, L.R., & Jansak, K.E. (2001). The ten keys to quality assurance and assessment in Online Learning. *Journal of Interactive Instruction Development, 13*(3), 3–18.

Bacow, L.S., Bowen, W.G., Guthrie, K.M., Lack, K.A., & Long, M.P. (2012). *Barriers to adoption of online learning systems in US higher education.* New York, NY: Ithaka S+ R.

Bartholomew, D. (2010). Colleges embrace online education. *Daily Breeze.* Retrieved from http://search.proquest.com/docview/755008217?accountid=25307.

Braude, S., & Merrill, J. (2013). The chancellor's new robes: Online education. *Creative Education, 4* (7A2), 50–52.

Breneman, D., Pusser, B., & Turner, S. (2006). *Earnings from learning: The rise of for-profit universities.* New York: State University of New York Press.

Beck, V.S. (2010). Comparing online and face to face teaching and learning. *Journal on Excellence in College Teaching, 21*(3), 95–108.

Bowen, W.G., & Lack, K.A. (2013). *Higher Education in the Digital Age.* New York, NY: Ithaka S+ R.

Bowen, W.G., & Tobin, E.M. (2015). *Locus of Authority: The Evolution of Faculty Roles in the Governance of Higher Education.* New York, NY: Ithaka S+ R.

Chickering, A.W., & Ehrmann, Z.F. (1997). *Seven Principles for Good Practice in Undergraduate Education.* Washington Center News. Retrieved from www.lonestar.edu/multimedia/sevenprinciples.pdf.

Diaz, D. (2002). Online drop rates revisited. Retrieved from http://ts.mivu.org/default.asp?show=article&id=981.

Fish, W.W., & Wickersham, L.E. (2009). Best practices for online instructors: Reminders. *The Quarterly Review of Distance Education, 10*(3), 279–284.

Frankola, K. (2001). Why online learners drop out. *Workforce, 80*(10), 53–59.

Gallien, T., & Oomen-Early, J. (2008). Personalized versus collective instructor feedback in the online course room: Does type of feedback affect student satisfaction, academic performance and perceived connectedness with the instructor? *International Journal on E-learning, 7*(3), 463–476.

Geiger, R.L. (2014). *The History of American Higher Education: Learning and Culture from the Founding to World War II.* Princeton: Princeton University Press.

Hansen, B. (2001). Distance Learning: Do Online Courses Provide a Good Education. CQ Researcher: *The Congressional Quarterly Inc.* Retrieved from http://photo.pds.org:5012/cqresearcher/getpdf.php?id=cqresrre2001120700.

Harting, K., & Erthal, M.J. (2005). History of distance learning. *Information Technology, Learning, and Performance Journal, 23*(1), 35–44.

Hiltz, S.R., & Goldman, R. (Eds.). (2004). *Learning Together Online: Research on Asynchronous Learning Networks.* Boston, MA: Routledge.

Means, B., Toyama, Y., Murphy, R., Bakia, M., & Jones, K. (2010). *Evaluation of Evidence-Based Practices in Online Learning: A Meta-analysis and Review of Online Learning Studies.* Washington DC: US Department of Education.

Neumann, P. (1998). Risks of E-education. *Communications of the ACM, 40,* 136.

Parker, K., Lenhart, A., & Moore, K. (2011). *The Digital Revolution and Higher Education: College Presidents, Public Differ on Value of Online Learning.* Pew Research Center: Pew Social and Demographic Trends.

Pianko, D., & Jarrett, J. (2012). Early days of a growing trend: Nonprofit/for-profit academic partnerships in higher education. In D. Oblinger (Ed.), *Game Changers: Education and Information Technologies* (pp. 91–104). Washington DC: Educause.

Quality Matters. (2015). Retrieved from www.qualitymatters.org.

Scheg, A.G. (2015). *Critical Examinations of Distance Education Transformation Across Disciplines.* Beaverton: Ringgold Inc. Retrieved from http://search.proquest.com/docview/1651933474?accountid=25307.

Twigg, C. (2001). *Quality Assurance for Whom? Providers and Consumers in Today's Distributed Learning Environment.* The Pew Learning and Technology Program, Center for Academic Transformation, Troy, New York. Retrieved from http://www.center.rpi.edu.

Yang, Y., & Cornelious, L.F. (2005). Preparing instructors for quality online instruction. *Online Journal of Distance Learning Administration, 8*(1).

CHAPTER 7

Leading Comprehensive Internationalization on Campus

Thimios Zaharopoulos

Introduction

Internationalization efforts on college campuses have been going on for quite a while with various levels of success. In most instances, such efforts have been defined as a way to attract international students to U.S. college campuses and/or study abroad opportunities for American students, as well as occasional area studies programs. However, internationalization is much more than that, and this article attempts to provide a concise roadmap to such efforts, currently defined as Comprehensive Internationalization (CI). The outline provided here aims to aid university management by offering examples of the practice and process of internationalization.

In an effort to broaden internationalization efforts, NAFSA has offered a definition of CI:

Comprehensive internationalization is a commitment, confirmed through action, to infuse international and comparative perspectives throughout the teaching, research, and service missions of higher education. It shapes institutional ethos and values and touches the entire higher education enterprise. It is essential that it be embraced by institutional leadership, governance, faculty, students, and all academic service and support units. It is an institutional imperative, not just a desirable possibility.

Comprehensive internationalization not only impacts all of campus life but the institution's external frames of reference, partnerships, and relations. The global reconfiguration of economies, systems of trade, research, and communication, and the impact of global forces on local life, dramatically expand the need for comprehensive internationalization and the motivations and purposes driving it (Hudzik, 2011).

ACE's (2012) Center for International and Global Engagement (CIGE) has outlined the following elements that make up CI (Figure 7.1):

I. *Articulated Institutional Commitment – Mission statements, strategic plans, and formal assessment mechanisms*

II. *Administrative Structure and Staffing – Reporting structures and staff and office configurations*

III. *Curriculum and co-curriculum, and learning outcomes – General education and language requirements, co-curricular activities and programs, and specified student learning outcomes*

IV. *Faculty policies and practices – Hiring guidelines, tenure and promotion policies, and faculty development opportunities*

V. *Student Mobility – Study abroad programs, and international student recruitment and support*

VI. *Collaboration and partnerships – Joint degree or dual/double-degree programs, branch campuses, and other offshore programs*

An added element of CI should be "Staff Policies and Practices." Students learn in and out of the classroom, and their lives are affected by both faculty and staff; therefore, staff needs to be part of a comprehensively internationalized institution.

This essay attempts to take the above definition and components of CI and show how to put them into practice by creating a CI plan.

Articulated Institutional Commitment

Any attempt to create a CI program starts with the institutional mission. Increasingly accrediting agencies focus on how institutions meet their stated mission and values, and their adherence to those values. If the mission statement does not formalize a commitment to internationalization and CI is only a "free-standing concept," it will not happen

(Hudzik & McCarthy, 2012). In some cases, even the inclusion of international elements in the mission statement will not mean much unless made explicit in the strategic plan.

Most institutions of higher education today have mission statements that include some type of reference to global or international presence or awareness. Increasingly mission and vision statements sound very similar. However, strategic plans do not necessarily follow up on the mission statements by promoting internationalization.

Even in cases where mission, vision statements and core values, as well as strategic plans include references to global education, relevant assessment mechanisms are missing, as dashboards usually rely on quantitative data such as enrollment, financial condition, and faculty-to-student ratios. Examples of mission statements that embrace internationalization include the following:

- *… University provides access to a quality higher education experience that prepares a diverse community of learners to think critically, communicate effectively, demonstrate a global perspective and …* (Park University).
- *It welcomes and seeks to serve persons of all racial, ethnic, and geographic groups, women and men alike, as it addresses the needs of an increasingly diverse population and a global economy* (Texas A& M).
- *… also aims, through public service, to enhance the lives and livelihoods of our students, the people of New York, and others around the world* (Cornell).
- *The university is dedicated to preparing its students for lives of learning and for the challenges educated citizens will encounter in an increasingly complex and diverse global community* (University of Kansas).

A number of colleges and universities include some reference to global citizenship or perspective as part of their core values:

- *… committed to providing knowledge and skills for life work that will promote the common good of humankind and lead to* *informed and principled participation in the global marketplace* (Bradley University).

- *Thinking locally and globally* (Union College)
- *Effective Global Citizenship* (The American College of Greece)
- *We challenge our students, faculty, staff and alumni to recognize their responsibility to improve the world around them, starting locally and expanding globally* (William Patterson University).

Such mission statements and values have to be reflected in the institutional strategic plan. It is the only way to ensure that the mission and values are carried out, as unlike mission statements, strategic plans are usually assessed.

A CI plan created for Park University was the result of an updated strategic plan, which called for internationalization activities. It started with a goal focused on student success, which included the aim of providing a "globally relevant education." One objective under that goal was the creation of a Global Institute. To make such goals assessable, the plan called for certain actions to be accomplished by a certain date. An example of a measurable objective was "50% of Park students participate in curricular and/or cocurricular programs and activities offered by, or in collaboration with the Global Institute." It additionally called for the creation of a CI plan, which would set targets for such things as the percentage of students who pursue Park's Global Proficiency Certificate.

Under the strategic plan's priority for "strengthening the brand," it included an objective that the university would be recognized as providing a "globally relevant education." A measurable related objective was that there would be a "10% increase annually in the number of students receiving recognition from external entities for activities related to internationalization or multiculturalism."

However, all strategic plans need to have formal assessment mechanisms, so that they do not remain only on paper. Most institutions use dashboards to present the progress of their strategic plans to their respective boards. However, every unit within that institution should report on an annual basis its progress toward meeting the strategic goals and objectives.

Administrative Structure and Staffing

A commitment to CI must be reflected in the administrative structure and staffing of the institution. At Park University the first step toward CI was the creation of the office of the Vice President of Global and Lifelong Learning, charged with drafting a CI plan and the strategy to internationalize the institution.

Nevertheless, the administration alone cannot take on the task of CI. There must be faculty input and buy-in. For this purpose, a faculty committee on international/multicultural education should exist to provide input, and deal with clearly academic issues related to internationalization, such as the curriculum.

Curriculum and Cocurriculum, and Learning Outcomes

The curriculum is the next important element of a CI plan. Without internationalizing the curriculum, the plan only involves incoming and outgoing students. This is an area that requires bold action.

Curriculum today can be discussed only in the context of competencies and learning outcomes. For example, starting with general education, are there specific global learning outcomes? Some institutions also have institutional learning goals that include international or global competencies.

Park University had established competencies (called "literacies") long before there was an attempt to internationalize the curriculum. However, the faculty and the deans worked together to add global learning competencies to the already existing ones. Under each of the categories, the faculty added at least one global learning outcome:

Global Learning Literacies
  1. *Analytical and Critical Thinking*
      1.5 *Synthesize knowledge gathered from different cultures in communication and problem-solving efforts.*
  2. *Community and Civic Responsibility*
      2.2 *Recognize the existence of diverse alternative systems and their necessary global relationships.*
      2.3 *Trace the geographical and historical roots which are shaping these systems.*

2.5 *Describe the diverse values, beliefs, ideas, and worldviews found globally into personal community and civic activities.*

3. **Scientific Inquiry**
   3.6 *Demonstrate understanding of the multicultural history and experimental nature of scientific knowledge.*

4. **Ethics and Values**
   4.3 *Recognize the diversity and similarities in value systems held by different cultures and co-cultures.*

5. **Literary and Artistic Expression**
   5.2 *Discuss diversities in the visual, verbal, and performing arts and the origins and reconciliation of such diversities.*
   5.3 *Compare and contrast the role of various art forms from a range of societies as both records and shapers of language and cultures.*

6. **Interdisciplinary and Integrative Thinking**
   6.2 *Synthesize diverse perspectives to achieve an interdisciplinary understanding.*
   6.3 *Discuss the relationships among academic knowledge, professional work, and the responsibilities of local and global citizenship.*

These competencies could serve as general education program outcomes, while individual majors could map their own program outcomes to the institutional or general education outcomes. It is imperative that specific measurable objectives and assessment methods are established in order to ensure that such outcomes are met. A few examples from Park University's CI plan related to program outcomes are listed here:

1. *Each academic program has a list of Core Competencies that students should meet before graduating with that specific degree.*
   Goals:
   a. *Ascertain how many of the degree programs, both graduate and undergraduate include at least one Core Competency that is directly tied to any of the Global Learning Literacies.*
   b. *By 2015, 75% of all academic programs will have at least one Core Competency that is directly tied to a Global Learning Literacy.*
2. *Each course at Park University has a list of approved Core Learning Outcomes (CLO), which are assessed via the Core Assessment.*

Goals:

a. *Ascertain how many of the Liberal Education (LE) courses include at least one CLO that is tied directly to any of the Global Learning Literacies.*

b. *Ascertain how many of the courses offered at Park University include at least one CLO that is tied directly to any of the Global Learning Literacies*

c. *By 2015, 75% of all LE courses will have at least one CLO that is directly tied to a Global Learning Literacy.*

d. *By 2016, 100% of all LE courses will have at least one CLO that is directly tied to a Global Learning Literacy.*

e. *By 2015, 50% of all Park courses will have at least one CLO that is directly tied to a Global Learning Literacy.*

f. *By 2017, 100% of all Park courses will have at least one CLO that is directly tied to a Global Learning Literacy.*

Cocurricular Activities

Internationalization can easily be inserted into the cocurricular activities offered to students (see Ward, 2014). These already take place at many institutions and include such things as an international festival, foreign film series, global friendship societies, international buddy system, and many more. Student affairs officers must take the lead in this area and organize activities that not only bring local students in contact with international students but also give all students opportunities to interact with and learn from each other and also interact with the greater community. In Kansas City, one of the city's largest festivals is the Ethnic Enrichment Festival, which brings over 50 different ethnic groups together to showcase their foods, music, and culture. Freshmen student orientation or some type of student engagement in such activities could easily be accomplished with very little cost.

Since learning takes place through such activities, they should also be assessed. A form of light assessment that some universities offer is an International Certificate for students who engage in international activities. This is similar to a more encompassing approach such as the Cocurricular Transcript that some institutions offer to students, listing their activities during their college years, and thus validating exposure to different ideas and practices, leadership behaviors, and other similar active engagement.

International experiences or global learning should be assessed as part of the normal learning assessment, provided global learning outcomes have been included at the program and/or course level, which many institutions do (Hill & Helms, 2013). Specific assessment tools for study abroad programs also exist, such as the Global Perspective Inventory (GPI), among other tools and rubrics (see Musil, 2006).

Faculty Policies and Practices

Policies and practices related to faculty internationalization efforts include hiring guidelines, tenure and promotion policies, and faculty development. Obviously, this is likely to be a difficult part of the program. However, if internationalization is a priority of the institution, then it must seek to hire faculty that fit this goal. The process can start by simply including the institutional mission statement on any job postings. That would inform prospective employees of the institutional priorities. Other actions in terms of hiring could take the form of noting desired candidate characteristics such as global research initiatives, internationalized courses, and international experiences, so that faculty and staff with such expertise are recruited and hired. During the interview process, some of the questions could be the degree to which a candidate's courses are internationalized, his or her international research agenda, and other international experiences.

Tenure and promotion criteria could give an extra edge to candidates for tenure and promotion that better fit the institutional mission and core values. At institutions where such criteria area numerical, extra points could be given to these international activities. Faculty development activities could include extra weight to sabbatical applications for work abroad, and of course, adequate funding for legitimate academic travel abroad.

Staff Policies and Practices

Although most documents about internationalization do not include much regarding non-teaching staff, evaluation criteria and especially training and professional development programs for staff should definitively include diversity awareness and training, and even travel abroad opportunities. At one institution, a staff member normally accompanies a faculty member to a service learning spring break program abroad. The only way for staff to handle issues of diversity and international students on campus, and to buy-in to the institutional mission is to get exposure and training. Quite often staff members have longer tenure at institutions than faculty and if they are not part of the program, academic efforts may be throated by complacency and bureaucracy.

Student Mobility

Under most circumstances, institutions usually think of internationalization in terms of receiving international students or sending students abroad. Obviously, in this era of difficult financial constraints, receiving international students has become a priority because of the additional income such students can bring. Besides bringing financial resources to the university, international students can facilitate global learning for local students. Experiences with international students in and out of the classroom help local students learn about differences and similarities with people unlike them. However, careful planning is needed to make sure that a desired balance is achieved not only in terms of the overall percentage of international students but also in terms of students of specific nationalities. Many colleges and universities recruit Chinese students. However, many in China do not look favorably at U.S. institutions that have an extraordinary number of Chinese students, and the more students from one nation the more likely they will interact only with each other; thus, the potential for their easier transition and global learning for local students is lost. Saudi authorities understand this and limit the number of Saudi students not only per U.S. college campus but also per major, and even per U.S. state.

Study abroad experiences for American students have always been a priority for colleges. Such experiences are invaluable and transformative educational tools. Study abroad can take various forms, such as short faculty led programs; college campuses abroad; or individual students going abroad to study. Many study abroad activities increasingly involve third-party providers.

In all cases, it is wise for local officials to visit foreign campuses before sending students there. The American College of Greece, for example, annually invites a handful of study abroad advisers to campus, so they can experience for a few days what their students would experience if they studied abroad there. A good way to facilitate study abroad is through exchange agreements, but this does not work for all institutions and all foreign institutions.

For both international and study abroad students, the most important element is "customer service," which is often missing. Students need a good orientation, personalized attention, and dedicated services. Students (and their parents) away from home need to feel that they will have all the help they need in a caring environment when away from home.

Collaboration and Partnerships

There is no denying that most interinstitutional Memorandums of Understanding (MOUs) stay filed and are never implemented. As such, careful research is needed in deciding the type of agreement to sign and with whom to sign it so that such partnerships are sustainable (Peterson, 2014).

Examples of such collaboration include exchange agreements, joint degree programs, dual-degree programs, branch campuses, and off shore programs (see Helms, 2012). It is beyond the scope of this article to deal with this huge subject. However, for such enterprises, institutions need to consult two sources: their regional accrediting agency for guidelines and their own strategic plans. For example, many potential partners in China would prefer that joint academic programs be done in Mandarin Chinese, which is almost impossible under many accrediting bodies. Very few schools have the ability or desire to create institutional networks such as NYU's network of campuses around the world. For smaller schools, other more creative ways may be needed. An example is the Global Liberal Arts Alliance (GLAA), a consortium of liberal arts colleges in the Great Lakes region and foreign liberal arts institutions working together to provide various types of experiences for their students.

Concluding Thoughts

CI reflects both an attitude and a set of behaviors and practices related to the contemporary needs of university management. It is made up of multiple elements, which are interrelated and whose foundation is an institutional commitment and most desired outcome is student learning.

CI is not just a desire but also a necessity, as quality education today inherently requires global learning. The best way to approach CI is through a commitment and an organized and assessable plan, which has buy-in by various constituencies, it reflects an investment by the institution, and sends a strong message that without global learning students will not be adequately prepared for a globalized environment. University management today cannot afford to ignore the need to internationalize and the best way to tackle this task is through a comprehensive manner.

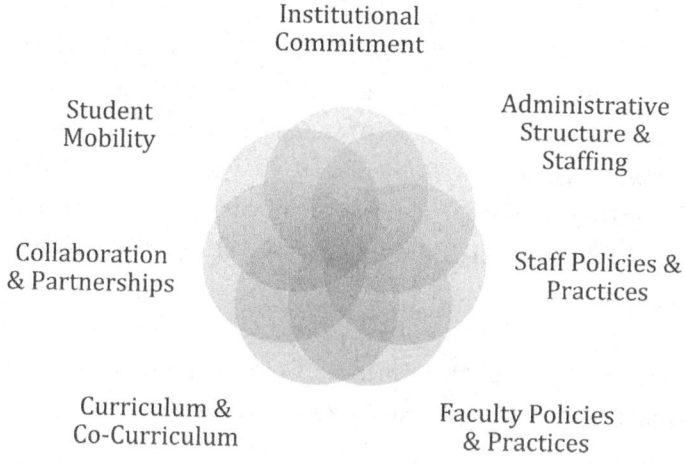

Figure 7.1 *Interrelated elements of comprehensive internationalization.*

References

ACE. (2012). *Mapping Internationalization on U.S. Campuses: 2012 Edition.* Washington, DC: American Council on Education. Retrieved from http://www.acenet.edu/news-room/Pages/2012-Mapping-Internationalization-on-U-S--Campuses.aspx.

Helms, R.M. (2012). *Mapping International Joint and Dual Degrees: U.S. Program Profiles and Perspectives.* Washington, DC: American

Council on Education. Retrieved from http://www.acenet.edu/news-room/Documents/Mapping-International-Joint-and-Dual-Degrees.pdf.

Hill, B.A., & Helms, R.M. (2013). *Leading the Globally Engaged Institution: New Directions, Choices, and Dilemmas - A Report from the 2012 Transatlantic Dialogue.* Washington, DC: American Council on Education. Retrieved from http://www.acenet.edu/news-room/Documents/CIGE-Insights-2013-Trans-Atlantic-Dialogue.pdf.

Hudzik, J.K. (2011). *Comprehensive Internationalization: From Concept to Action: Executive Summary.* Washington, DC: NAFSA.

Hudzik, J.K., & McCarthy, J.S. (2012). *Leading Comprehensive Internationalization: Strategy and Tactics for Action.* Washington, DC: NAFSA. Retrieved from http://www.d.umn.edu/vcaa/intz/-NAFSA_Leading%20Comprehensive%20Internationalization.pdf.

Musil, C.M. (2006). *Assessing Global Learning: Marching Good Intentions with Good Practice.* Washington, DC: AAC&U. Retrieved from http://archive.aacu.org/SharedFutures/documents/Global_Learning.pdf.

Peterson, P.M., & Helms, R.M. (2014). *Challenges and Opportunities for the Global Engagement of Higher Education.* Washington, DC: American Council on Education. Retrieved from http://www.acenet.edu/news-room/Documents/CIGE-Insights-2014-Challenges-Opps-Global-Engagement.pdf.

Ward, H.H. (2014). *Internationalizing the Co-curriculum: A 3-Part Series.* Washington, DC: American Council on Education. Retrieved from http://www.acenet.edu/news-room/Pages/Internationalization-in-Action.aspx.

CHAPTER 8

Global Higher Education: A Perspective from Spain

Fernando Galván

Introduction

The aim of this article is to present some ideas and data about the role that Spain can play in the global world of higher education, particularly in connection with two continents to which Spain has been historically attached, that is, Europe and Latin America. Spain is now a mid-size country, with a population between 46 and 47 million people. Since 1986 it is part of the European Union and, for historical and cultural reasons, it plays an important role in Europe and prides itself on an impressive artistic and cultural heritage, which dates back to Roman and Medieval times and is particularly rich in the Modern Age. But in addition to this deep European heritage, Spain is also a country with very close relations with Latin America, as large areas of the American territory were conquered and colonized by Spaniards during the 16th and 17th centuries.

Spain's Academic Reach

As a result of that, some 20 countries in Latin America and the Caribbean speak Spanish and share many cultural traits with Spain. The figures are illustrative: about 430 million people speak Spanish as their mother tongue worldwide, including some 50 million in the United States (usually bilingual speakers of Latin American origin who speak regularly both English and Spanish) (Instituto Cervantes, 2013; Galván, 2014b).

Spanish is thus the mother tongue of more people than those who have English as their native language, although English is of course the international *lingua franca*, with a total of about 1.5 billion speakers in the world; Spanish is spoken only by a total of about 500 million, counting both native speakers and those who use it as a second or foreign language. That is mainly why the role Spain plays in the world of culture and education is not only restricted to Europe, but it is largely also one that extends to America (particularly Latin America), and is gradually spreading every day to other areas of the world, such as the United States, Asia, and Africa.

The University in Spain has a long history, closely linked to the development of the European university, and some of the current Spanish universities, notably Salamanca, Valladolid, and Alcalá, are among the oldest in Europe. The first Higher Education Institutions (HEIs), then called in Latin *Studium Generale* (*General Study*), were established in the late 11th century: Bologna is credited as the oldest one, being created in 1089, soon followed by Oxford around 1096. Others were founded during the 12th century, such as the *Studium Generale* of Paris in 1150, and still others came later, like Cambridge, whose establishment took place in the 13th century, around 1209. In Spain, the oldest universities that have survived to our days date, like Cambridge, from the 13th century: Salamanca in 1218, Valladolid around 1241, and Alcalá in 1293. All these universities, and others, flourished particularly in the Modern Age, and some of them projected their educational models to America. As is well known, the English and Scottish universities were the models followed in the erection of colleges like those at Harvard (1636), or in what is now Canada, and of course the Universities of Alcalá and Salamanca were taken as models of universities in Latin America, like those founded in the 16th century in Santo Domingo (Dominican Republic), Mexico or Peru, among many others.

The Spanish University system now consists of 82 institutions, 50 of them public and 32 private universities (Conferencia de Rectores de Universidades Españolas, 2013; Ministerio de Educación, Cultura y Deporte, 2014). Most of the latter have been established in the last 20 years, which means that the public system is predominant in Spain. A public university receives between 60% and 70% of its budget from public funding, either directly or indirectly (through competitive funding for research for instance); the private institutions, however, can only receive public funding under competitive basis for research. The total number of University students is now a little over 1.5 million, 85% of whom pursue their studies at public universities (Ministerio de Educación, Cultura y Deporte, 2014).

Many of these 82 Spanish universities are also part of the European University Association (EUA), which comprises approximately 850 HEIs from 47 countries, and 17 million students. Because of the existing close links among many universities in Europe, not only through EUA but also by means of other consortiums and common ventures in the EHEA (European Higher Education Area), which includes universities from countries outside the EU, it is no wonder that many European students come to Spanish universities and that many Spaniards pursue their studies at other European HEIs. The best known program for mobility of students and staff in Europe is the Erasmus Program, which has been active since 1987. This program has been very successful so far: during these last 25 years nearly 3 million students have enjoyed academic stays at European universities other than their own for at least one semester, and also more than 300,000 members of faculty and staff have moved to universities in 33 European countries, with public funding from EU and national and regional governments. Within this context, Spanish universities have proved the most active in recent times, to the extent that Spain is now the country with the greatest number of incoming European students (39,300 in the academic year 2012–2013), and outgoing Spanish students to EU universities (39,545 in the same academic year) (Ministerio de Educación, Cultura y Deporte, 2014).

Internationalization of Spanish Institutions

Most of the European students who come to Spain do so from the largest countries in Europe such as Italy, France, Germany, and the United Kingdom. Some percentages will help understand what is happening: 35% of Italian students under the Erasmus Program come to Spanish universities; for Britain the percentage is 23%; for France, 22%; and for Germany, 20%. Other smaller countries also send a considerable number of their Erasmus students to Spanish universities: that is the case for Belgium, Cyprus, and Portugal, for instance, with similar percentages to those just mentioned: between 20% and 25%. Ireland, The Netherlands, Poland, and Slovenia send, each of them, nearly 20% of their

Erasmus students to Spain. The most popular destinations for Spanish students who go to other European universities are countries such as Italy (22%), France (13%), Germany (11%), and the UK (11%) (European Commission, 2012).

These figures and percentages show the map of relationships and contacts established between Spanish universities and their counterparts in Europe. However, it is important to realize that not only students under the umbrella of the Erasmus Program are concerned, but also faculty and studies. An increasingly cooperative academic and research activity is being developed: joint undergraduate and graduate degrees, collaboration in research projects, joint supervision of doctorates, shared authorship of research papers, etc. The picture provided so far is the one supplied by the most recent figures available (academic year 2012–2013), but the perspective for coming years is certainly more favorable; now the EHEA (also known familiarly as "Bologna agreements") is fully implemented in almost all European countries. What is to be expected for the future is an increase in this collaborative work between Spanish and other European universities and the development of common degrees and consortiums of HEIs. In this respect, research European programs, such as the new Horizon 2020 (H2020) will naturally boost this at the research level, since the budget for H2020 is nearly €80 billion for the period 2014–2020, addressed mainly to joint proposals (presented by at least three universities from three different countries) to improve scientific excellence, industrial and innovation leadership, and social challenges (Galván, 2014a).

However, as remarked earlier, the academic links for Spanish universities are global. The association with Latin American universities is so strong that many more students come to Spanish universities from Latin America than those who come from other European countries, especially for Graduate Studies, which have a clear influence on research and innovation. Some basic figures follow: although the percentage of foreign students at Spanish universities is still very low (nearly 5% in the last academic year), what is remarkable is that in the case of undergraduates the percentage is extremely low (about 3.7%), whereas for Masters the percentage goes up to 18.4%. Even more remarkable is the origin of those international students. This is shown in Tables 8.1 and 8.2.

Table 8.1 Percentages of International Undergraduate Students in Spain

EU-27	41.4%
Latin American	29.5%
Northern Africa	8.9%
Rest of Europe	8.5%
Asia-Pacific	8.4%
Rest of Africa	2.6%
United States and Canada	0.9%

Table 8.2 Percentages of International Graduate Students (Masters Degrees) in Spain

Latin American	53.7%
EU-27	20.8%
Asia-Pacific	13.5%
Rest of Europe	4.9%
United States and Canada	3.4%
Northern Africa	2.3%
Rest of Africa	1.6%

These figures show very clearly how much the Spanish university system is already contributing to the development of Latin American higher education, particularly in the training of graduate and PhD students, as the lack of faculty with Masters and PhD degrees is perceived by many universities in Latin America as their main current weakness.

Implications of Spain's Academic Initiatives

The governments of some countries have now established programs with substantial funding in order to alleviate this situation, like Brazil through its "Science without Boundaries" program, or Colombia, Ecuador, and Chile. Other international private organizations, such as Banco Santander through its Universia programs, have launched initiatives to foster mobility for graduate students and internships in industries and in small- and medium-sized companies (Galván, 2014a; Galván, 2014b). It is true that not all actions in these programs are concerned exclusively with Spain, because other countries are also eligible (mainly the United States and other European countries), but the common language and cultural traits between Spain and many of these Latin American countries constitute undoubtedly a powerful pole of attraction toward Spanish universities.

Thus, over the next 20 years, at least Spanish and Latin American universities will face numerous challenges in training, mobility, scientific development, international presence, visibility, and dissemination, which may have a great impact globally. Although it is true that many universities around the world have recently begun to incorporate training their students in English, particularly at the graduate level, this tendency has not yet extended widely through Spain and Latin America. This is probably due to the fact that more than a thousand universities worldwide and large sectors of the world population use Spanish, not English, for everyday communication. It seems self-evident that such an important asset cannot be ignored and that Spanish and Latin American universities are not necessarily to act as if they were Norwegian, Dutch, German, or Polish universities, whose native languages are rarely spoken outside their national frontiers, that is, for universities outside the English-speaking countries, there seems to be little (if any) alternative other than using English if they want to be globally relevant, if they wish to attract international talent and innovation.

However, even if obviously Spanish cannot compete in numbers or international presence with English, for a language spoken by some 500 million people in more than 20 countries the situation looks somewhat different to those other languages spoken by a few million people in limited territories. Let us consider not only that Spanish is a language known and spoken in Spain and Latin America, and in some places in Africa as well, but also that the United States has a population of Hispanic origin, which is now over 50 million people, and which will quite probably (if the statistics are correct) easily reach a hundred million by mid-century. There are in fact hundreds of colleges and universities in the United States where an important number of students and faculty use Spanish on a daily basis. Evidence of this is the influential "Hispanic Association of Colleges and Universities" (HACU) (Instituto Cervantes & British Council, 2011).

Concluding Thoughts

The consequences of this situation will probably be, if sufficient funding be allocated by the governments of the countries involved and also by industries and multinational organizations, that more mobility programs will come into effect for both undergraduate and graduate students between Latin American and Spanish universities. This is undoubtedly a major challenge for the social and economic development of many Latin American countries, as they are in urgent need of highly qualified professionals in all the productive sectors and in education. Training these highly qualified professionals in the main Latin American and Spanish Universities is an objective that may be more easily achieved, in a relatively short time, if academic recognition programs are implemented for their undergraduate studies and if mobility is promoted toward the most competitive graduate schools within the Spanish-speaking world. There are universities in Argentina, Chile, Colombia, Mexico, Spain, and other countries, that, without a shadow of doubt, could make a significant contribution to this mission (Galván, 2014b).

The economic development and spread of many large multinational companies throughout Latin America and Spain provide a rare opportunity for universities, and governments, to reach agreements with these supranational companies and organizations to offer undergraduate and graduate students professional work placements and internships. This would allow students to maximize and complete their university training, while giving also the opportunity to companies and organizations to benefit from highly qualified human assets, students who speak the language of the country and would have no particular difficulties adapting to the culture. Clearly, the advantages are quite evident not only for companies but also for university students, who would acquire professional experience in international centers and organizations, and, of course, for universities, which would extend their educational and intellectual leadership to the productive sector, thereby enriching their graduates' knowledge and future employability.

Research and innovation, which are mainly developed at the university in most of these countries, would also benefit from these sorts of initiatives. While Latin American and Spanish universities have agreements that allow researchers to cooperate and participate in exchanges, these agreements could surely be extended, if the respective governments so wish, to other public research organizations. This would facilitate the so-called Ibero-American Knowledge Space ("Espacio Iberoamericano del Conocimiento") by allowing and encouraging the best research groups to cooperate, the coauthoring of scientific works, the publication of scientific periodicals in Spanish, cooperation in business, and technical development. All of the above, evidently, would contribute to the socioeconomic development of these countries and boost greater wealth and prosperity for their citizens (Galván, 2014a).

Spanish-speaking universities, like all those that do not work in English, have an important deficit in indexed journals in Journal Citation Reports (JCR), to the extent that much research that is not published in English does not receive due attention, owing to the low impact of the journals in which it is published. This is immediately apparent if we consult the data: in 2011, 97% of the journals in JCR were published in English, compared with the modest 1.18% in Spanish. It would clearly be unrealistic to think that this data could be changed in the next decades; however, measures might be implemented to improve the situation in specific fields such as the *Social Sciences and Humanities* journals, where the percentages are slightly higher. A coherent policy, then, to encourage synergies in these areas in the Spanish-speaking context could increase the number of *Social Sciences* journals, which appear in JCR: 81 journals in 2010 (47 in Spain, 10 in Mexico, 9 in Chile, 6 in Colombia, 4 in Argentina, 3 in Venezuela, and 1 in Brazil and another in the United States), representing 2.97% of the indexed journals in this field (from a total of 2,731 journals, 2,384 were published in English, in other words 87.29%). Spanish is the second language in which most *Social Sciences* journals appear in JCR, despite the enormous gap compared with English. Boosting studies in this field in Spanish, through university coordination and cooperation, would undoubtedly bolster these publications, thereby contributing to expanding and foregrounding the Ibero-American Knowledge Space globally more effectively (García Delgado, Alonso & Jiménez, 2013; Galván, 2014b).

Hence, if not in other spheres, at least in Humanities and Social Sciences, Spanish-speaking universities do have a role to play on a global scale, and a mission to implement in the coming decades, provided greater cooperation through the measures described above can be achieved. Not only intergovernmental agreements will be necessary, but also bilateral and multilateral cooperation and exchanges between other public and private international organizations, such as, among others, the SEGIB (Secretaría General Iberoamericana), the EU-LAC Foundation, CAF-Development Bank of Latin America, the IAUP (International Association of University Presidents), and the Santander-Universia initiative.

References

Conferencia de Rectores de Universidades Españolas. (2013). *La universidad española en cifras 2012.* Madrid: CRUE.

European Commission. (2012). *Erasmus –Facts, Figures & Trends. The European Union Support for Student and Staff Exchanges and University Cooperation in 2010-11.* Luxemburg: Publications Office of the European Union.

Galván, F. (2014a). Docencia e investigación universitarias en el ámbito iberoamericano. *Cuadernos hispanoamericanos, 769–770* (July–August), 39–50.

Galván, F. (2014b). Un espacio de excelencia en español. *Nueva Revista de Política, Cultura y Arte, 151,* 347–358.

García Delgado, J.L., Alonso, J.A., & Jiménez, J.C. eds. (2013). *El español, lengua de comunicación científica.* Madrid & Barcelona: Fundación Telefónica & Ariel.

Instituto Cervantes. (2013). *El español en el mundo. Anuario del Instituto Cervantes 2013.* Madrid: Instituto Cervantes.

Instituto Cervantes & British Council. (2011). *Word for Word. The Social, Economic and Political Impact of Spanish and English / Palabra por palabra. El impacto social, económico y político del español y del inglés.* Madrid: Instituto Cervantes, British Council & Editorial Santillana.

Ministerio de Educación, Cultura y Deporte. (2014). *Datos y cifras del sistema universitario español.* Madrid: Gobierno de España.

PART 2

Leading the Way

CHAPTER 9

Never Alone: Building an Effective Management Team

Gary A. Dill

Introduction

Educators who become university presidents are often optimistic, positive, forward thinking leaders who confidently anticipate the responsibilities of the position. Only a misguided, naïve, or arrogant university president would attempt to conduct the day-to-day business of a modern university alone. Even the most visionary, iconic, individual educational leader recognizes the need to build an effective management team. The *AGB Task Force on the State of the Presidency in American Higher Education, The Leadership Imperative* (Association of Governing Boards of Universities and Colleges, 2006), utilized the term "integral leadership" to describe the process of tying the "strands of presidential responsibility" together and being "capable of course corrections as new challenges emerge" (p. vii). Most presidents of institutions of higher education recognize that recruiting and nurturing a senior leadership team consisting of the chief administrators of each of the various major components of the educational enterprise is the way to "tie the separate strands" and lead the institution effectively.

Very effective management teams are composed of multitalented, ethically focused, and highly motivated leaders who are able to work well together. At times, a leader seeking to build a management team is able to observe talented, ethical, motivated managers within an organization who demonstrate administrative abilities evidenced by a record of wise decision making. At other times, positions become vacant under circumstances requiring an external search and identification process. In either case, assembling an effective leadership team presents significant opportunities and challenges.

Embracing the Mission

Articulating clearly the well-defined mission of a college or university is the critically important initial step in determining an appropriate administrative structure and the attributes sought in the individuals who will comprise an effective management team. In 2002, when College of the Southwest (now University of the Southwest) inaugurated a new president, the institution faced significant challenges. While the previous president had led a heroic, Herculean effort for more than a decade to strengthen a fragile institution that had faced the real possibility of having to close its doors, the small college struggled. Located in the Permian Basin in southeast New Mexico, the institution served the local community primarily as a degree-completion opportunity for adult learners who returned to higher education in mid-life seeking to enhance employment opportunities by achieving a baccalaureate degree. With an improving economy, the small institution of higher education faced a dwindling local student base as employment opportunities improved across the economic spectrum.

The institution's Board of Trustees employed a new president who could build on the strengths of the retiring president who had firmly established the institution's appeal and benefit to the local constituency. The new vision anticipated an enhanced academic program that could add a significant number of traditional aged students to supplement the dwindling number of nontraditional local students. Accomplishing this would involve significant enhancement to the physical plant by adding residential facilities, student life recreational and physical educational resources, and expanding the number of well-prepared faculty members.

After inaugurating the new president, a comprehensive process that included trustees, faculty, staff, students, and alumni to consider carefully the way in which the institutional mission was framed and communicated. Although the process revealed wide spread support for the college's stated purpose, the board approved a restatement of the institutional mission with explicitly stated guidelines that succinctly framed the mission.

University of the Southwest is a Christ-centered educational community dedicated to developing men and women for a lifetime of servant leadership by emphasizing individual faith, responsibility, and initiative.

- *Teaching at University of the Southwest adheres to belief in God, in the Bible as the inspired Word of God, in Jesus Christ as the Son of God, and in the separation of church and state.*
- *University of the Southwest strives for excellence in academic curriculum, campus life programming, and student activities in a supportive educational community where freedom of thought and expression is honored and the demonstration of faith in acts of service is encouraged;*
- *At University of the Southwest, students are instructed and mentored by a faculty and staff who demonstrate Christ-centered values and maintain an environment where students can live and work cooperatively, valuing the multiple cultures from which they come; and*
- *As a community of initiative, University of the Southwest challenges graduates to become enterprising members of our society contributing to the common good by advocating and participating in the productive commerce of free enterprise, the constitutional privilege of self-government, and the practical contributions of community service. (https://www.usw.edu/About-USW/Mission)*

As a result of this mission clarifying process, although some members of the faculty and staff determined that they would be unable to support the newly clarified mission and left the college's employment, more than 90% of the faculty and staff remained. All of these and each newly hired faculty and staff member embraced fully the mission statement as a condition of continuing employment.

The president then conferred with the senior leadership and constituted them as an administrative team that would guide the institution in accomplishing its freshly articulated mission. The administrative team includes the chief academic officer, the chief financial officer, the chief student services officer, the chief advancement officer, and the campus steward—each of whom reports directly to the president. While the titles and numbers of such positions vary among institutions, such a cabinet-like administrative entity composed of senior administrators usually serves an institution of higher education. Critically important for the University of the Southwest (USW) was identifying a team of administrators who could provide exemplary leadership with an unequivocal voice.

Individual Voices—One United Message

Whether framed as the Latin phrase *Unus pro omnibus, omnes pro uno* (all for one, one for all), the traditional motto of Switzerland, inverted as *Un pour tous, tous pour un* (one for all, all for one), the motto traditionally associated with the three heroes of the classic novel, *The Three Musketeers* (Dumas, 1844), or as the United States motto *e pluribus unum* (from many, one), the challenge of forging a united message from strong individual contributors can be formidable. Each of the individual team members needs to have the appropriate levels of academic preparation and professional experience to meet established criteria for senior administrative leadership. Yet, finding the correct "fit" for each position involves an artful assurance of academic and professional qualification with personal disposition and proven ability to work as a cooperative team member.

For each position, highly qualified, experienced professionals are needed who have received appropriate graduate academic degrees; who have records of demonstrating successful, cooperative leadership; and who are confident people secure enough personally and professionally to participate vigorously in institutional decision making. At the same time, such highly qualified professionals need the ability to embrace fully a decision that had been carefully achieved, even when the conclusion to the decision making process does not fully represent the perspective of the individual administrator. Ideally, each member of the administrative team is thoroughly qualified to accomplish every aspect of her or his position description; is able to speak clearly and succinctly to the merits of an issue; and is at the same time able to participate cooperatively in achieving and communicating compromise.

Distinctive Institutional Characteristics

The faith-based nature of the USW mission constitutes a critical component of the lens through which each senior administrator is perceived. Aspiring to foster a "Christ-centered educational community dedicated to developing men and women for a lifetime of servant leadership by emphasizing individual faith, responsibility, and initiative" affords a special opportunity to emphasize to potential senior administrators the importance of aspiring to be models of responsible servant leaders, who reflect the importance of institutionally embraced values when acting in administrative roles.

Practically, the faith-based nature of the institution without any denominational or other religious body affiliation provides an additional opportunity to underscore the importance of fostering a cooperative environment that celebrates diversity of perspective. Being an integral and constructive part of the USW administrative team is best accomplished by people who value supportive, spirited, and civil discourse while recognizing that honest disagreeing about important matters. For example, the chief academic officer might argue passionately that a particular academic program ought to be initiated, contending that the program will enhance the quality of many existing programs while offering splendid opportunities for faculty members to integrate further mission-focused values in the curriculum. When the chief financial officer responds by requesting projections of potential revenue that would be required to make such an addition financially viable, a lively constructive conversation might ensue in which all of these factors and more are discussed vigorously with all senior administrators engaging in the dialogue. The most helpful administrative team is able to communicate clearly and passionately while discussing an issue and deciding a course of action. Then, when a decision is reached—whether a compromise endorsed by all or a conclusion enunciated by the president informed by the perspectives of respected colleagues who differ substantially on a desired outcome—the entire team is able to embrace the decision unanimously.

A Cabinet for Communication

Perhaps as important as having a cohesive mission-guided administrative team to lead an institution of higher education is fostering a culture of communication that keeps internal and external constituents adequately informed. As a supplement to the Administrative Team, the president of USW formed a larger "cabinet" that composed the student body president, the chair of the faculty, deans of each of the university's three schools, and direct reports of the senior administrators who served as a forum, which met regularly (at least monthly) to encourage and enhance communication on the campus. The university president chairs the meetings and agenda items that can be proposed by any cabinet member. In addition to hearing regular reports on enrollment, recruiting, and student activities, the communication cabinet served as a way for senior administrators to communicate administrative decisions convey budgetary information and provide input and feedback about various issues related to institutional policy and governance.

Conclusion

In summary, assembling an effective management team requires a visionary leader who can identify very talented professionals of unwavering ethical principles who are united in a commitment to accomplish a clearly articulated mission. An administrative team consisting of the chief administrative officers of each of the major structural divisions provides an opportunity for a coordinated and cohesive institutional governance structure. Each senior administrator should have the academic qualifications and professional experiences expected in a well-regarded university. Each senior administrator should have sufficient self-confidence and awareness to participate vigorously in team discussions advocating for speaking against issues in a way that reflects informed professionalism. Each senior administrator should be committed unequivocally to the established institutional mission. Each member of the administrative team should be committed to supporting fully institutional decisions that ultimately emerge as the result of principled discussions. Adequate mechanisms are required to communicate clearly with all institutional constituents.

References

Association of Governing Boards of Universities and Colleges. (2006). *The Leadership Imperative: The Report of the AGB Task Force on the State of the Presidency in American Higher Education.* Washington, DC: Association of Governing Boards of Universities and Colleges.

Dumas, A. (1844). *The Three Musketeers.* p. 112. Available at: http://www.literaturepage.com/read/thethreemusketeers.html

USW. (2015). University of the Southwest, Hobbs, New Mexico. Available at: https://www.usw.edu/About-USW/Mission

CHAPTER 10

Creating and Sustaining the University Leadership Pipeline

Don Betz

Leadership education, recruitment, and development are essential to the university's short- and long-term viability and success.

How does a university and those responsible for guiding it, ensure its continuing growth and development? In what ways does the institution consciously enhance its future through the shaping of processes and persons each ready and able to contribute to institutional relevance, vitality, and success?

How do a newly selected president and the Board that appoints him/her clearly delineate the importance of this leadership development role, not only for current management/staff but for those early in their careers? How is intentionality regarding leadership development established and then clearly communicated and demonstrated to the various campus constituencies? How will we know when this commitment to growing leadership achieves sufficient acceptance that it becomes a recognized tenet of institutional culture?

What are the necessary and sufficient conditions required for the establishment and the growth of the leadership talent "pipeline"? What values should guide current leadership in this process? What of the use of role models within and outside the institution? How does leadership pipeline development become a university priority, one that transcends the service of a particular president and other senior leaders and managers?

Growing university leadership talent must be intentional. Institutional success is dependent in large measure on the quality and depth of its leadership pool. As it is true for society, so it is for the institution that "human talent is the only true sustainable resource." The consistent cultivating of individual talent to assume various leadership roles throughout the institution is a primary responsibility of the president and senior leadership. Key principles, practices, and attitudes must be inextricably interwoven to create a culture supportive of this essential developmental process. Building a viable, collaborative, successful team requires vision and patience, an acute sense of the individual and collective talents that comprise an effective team, and an active recognition that leadership teams are not simply a cluster of personal agendas and aspirations linked by an interest only in personal success. Walter Issacson, CEO of the Aspen Institute, concludes in *The Innovators* "creating a team of competence is harder than creating the idea or product."

Principles

One of the keys to successful team building and, importantly, to extending that priority throughout the university and into the future, is the common commitment to a shared vision, mission, and values. Beyond the daily demands and expected academic processes, the president and the institution must create a bond, a firm connection among leaders and managers at each level within the institution. An articulated sense of purpose, enunciated infrequently and confined to a few senior leaders, will not effectively transmit the unifying sense of purpose across the institution. Further, the institutional imperative to create and sustain the generation of fresh leadership talent over time will fail if not embraced by the current leadership team. It is not easy to identify and adhere to a goal whose actual accomplishment is to be achieved in the future. But, if the goal is, in fact, realized, then the university benefits are substantive and culture-shaping.

The vision should capture the essence of the university's identity in a dynamic manner and be an expression of genuine institutional values. It should ground the institution in the place and people it serves. The team, faculty, and staff will accept and embrace that vision if it is a consistent, and sometimes inspirational, expression of the rationale for pursuing this work. Kouzes and Posner always include the ability to "inspire a shared vision" in their several works on leadership and credibility. The vision can galvanize the varied university constituencies around the objectives, and keep their "eye on the prize," if the publicly articulated vision also finds resonance in the individual's personal values. The university vision becomes the professional and personal *raison d'etre* for the campus community expressed in a most compelling and transparent manner.

This shared perspective is essential as institutions and their leaders continually adjust to the relentless, unforgiving challenge of change. The breadth and depth of disruptive intrusion permeates our world, our lives, and our institutions from every imaginable direction. Thomas Friedman has been chronicling this pattern of growth and change now at an accelerated pace unimagined just a few years ago when he wrote *The World Is Flat.* He notes that Facebook, Twitter, and Skype have all emerged as global phenomena transforming human connection in the last 7 years. Further, he speaks of a revolutionary threshold occurring in the next 5 years when "every person on the planet, if they have the motivation, will be on the network via a smart device." These devices are found in every country and in the hands of young and old alike, from Chicago to Chengdu, from Gaza to Gambia.

The guideposts for stability (and sanity) amid this protracted turbulence lie, at least in part, in the quality of leadership and the enthusiasm for the shared purpose. If we don't understand "what we are doing here," it will be almost impossible for universities and colleges to survive change relevant, and intact. The vision is set onto the foundation of institutional values and guides the successive leadership teams through the inevitable and necessary, multiple mid-course corrections. Thus, in the organization, there is an inextricable interconnection between mission, vision and values, and the presidents and senior university leaders' patterns of effective messaging.

Many team members will remain at the institution, and continue to learn, mature, and contribute to the university's vitality if they feel valued. Investment in a succession of key mid-level leaders and rising stars is fundamental to long-term institutional dynamism and stability. Encouragement is one of several potent tools perceptive leaders employ to consistently message that the individual is central to actualizing the university mission via its strategic plan and deep-seeded, community-wide collaboration. Tangible evidence of his/her value is the institution's consistent willingness to invest in his/her professional growth and development. This affirmation can assume many forms, from focused educational opportunities, including support for pursuing advanced/specialized degrees, focused training, unique short-term assignments, to representing the university in a variety of public forums, service on local and state boards of community partners, among others.

In this way, the president demonstrably messages confidence in current senior team members' commitment and competence, and, significantly, in others with currently more limited responsibilities. Such attention can result in sustained loyalty and connection to the institution and its mission when alternative opportunities appear for some as "shiny objects" on the horizon. From experience, it is clear that the university community is aware of these actions, which reinforce the salience of the vision. The stability of the mission and the message is recognized as an assurance of continuing opportunity for those who may desire to enter the university leadership preparation pipeline.

The president and senior leadership must "model the way" (Kouzes & Posner, 2012; *The Leadership Challenge*) on collaborative practices. A president's intentions and actions are writ large across the university community landscape, and those so disposed will be monitoring for any gaps between those intentions and actions. If such occur, and they can even with the best of intentions, then a "coterie of the watchful" will be looking to determine whether the actions were an aberration from the stated path or perhaps a confirmation of their unspoken suspicions. Consistency and openness can be effective in dissipating any doubts of the leadership's true intentions.

Collaborative leadership, inspired and anchored squarely at the top levels of organizational management, is one of the transformational characteristics of institutions deliberately building its future. David Brooks (*New York Times*, December 17, 2014), who regularly offers insight on the broad range of political and social issues, depicts collaboration as an art far too scarce among leaders, from global to local. "You can spot the collaborative leader because he's rejected the heroic, solitary model of leadership. He doesn't try to dominate his organization as its all-seeing visionary, leading idea generator and controlling intelligence.

Instead, he sees himself as a stage-setter, a person who makes it possible for the creativity in his organization to play itself out. The collaborative leader lessens the power distance between himself and everybody else."

The collaborative leader sets broad goals based on institutional values and skillful discernment of the current milieu and where and whom the university serves. He/she proceeds in concert with others whose experience, expertise, insight, and instincts he/she values. Such value has either been demonstrated over time, or is evidenced in the promise a particular team member demonstrates. He/she might not be the most seasoned member of the team, but he/she demonstrates the proclivity toward understanding the issues confronting the institution, and he/she contributes to the interactive deliberations in fresh and clarifying ways. He/she is not an echo of a colleague's comments, attempting to gain attention by speaking out often, but rather listens in an absorptive manner and then offers new ideas and useful context.

Practices

Effectively recruiting for the institution's leadership team and pipeline is one of the president's salient and continuing responsibilities. He/she shares this duty for leadership vitality and continuity with selected members of the current leadership team.

The intention must be clear and transparent. It should be understood as an institutional priority that transcends the tenure of the president. Therefore, the president must position this obligation deep within the institution, consistently and over time, so that it earns an accepted place in the shared values and objectives of the university. Through continuing interaction with the Cabinet and senior leadership, supported by the president's public statements, this organizational practice can earn a place in the institution's culture.

This investment in the university's leadership pipeline is reinforced by an equal enthusiasm for the growth of the senior team members. Beyond personal encouragement, the president actively sponsors mid-level and senior leaders to advance their knowledge and skills via conference and programs in which they actively participate and return with the harvest of information and insight to be shared formally and informally, with colleagues. The president leads by example by relating the substance and insights gleaned from meetings and conferences. Other team members will benefit from this example, and they can be tasked to connect with both peers and their own team members, and therefore amplify the impact of the invested resources by sharing what they learned. This strategy can become a study in efficiency and effectiveness.

A pivotal dimension of a successful strategy is nurturing an environment conducive to trust and support among the president's team members. Integrity and clarity are critical ingredients in creating and sustaining the team and its members. President and General Dwight D. Eisenhower counseled "The supreme quality for leadership is unquestionably integrity. Without it, no real success is possible." For trust, or lack of it, will be one of the consequences of the group's dynamic connection, and those intertwined relationships, whether observed from a distance, or up close and daily, can directly influence those who may decide to seek entry into the university's leadership pipeline.

The quality of the senior team's relationships, namely, their support for one another, in public or private, can also determine their collective success.

The evidence of such mutually supportive relationships is not lost on the university community. Many on campus search for the fissures among those in management/leadership positions either to exploit the disequilibrium for private gain, or as affirmation that they need not heed the strategy and planning promoted by the senior team. One could easily overhear comments to the effect that "If they do not support one another, why should we embrace the 'plan du jour'?" A divided "leadership" team can render institutional aspirations DOA.

Further, such division can become a debilitating deterrent to rising talent. He/she observes this absence of camaraderie, or worse, and concludes not to seek leadership opportunities, or at least not at that institution. Whether these interpersonal interactions among the leadership team members are overt and stark, or subtle and nuanced, they can eventually, and effectively, corrode the cultural basis upon which the mission and vision are founded, and, importantly, the unified sense of purpose that is conducive to producing exceptional outcomes. Why would a fresh talent aspire to join a siloed "team of rivals"? In such a scenario, one outcome is almost inevitable. The leadership pipeline will either be empty, or filled with some aspirants who may regard the "culture of division" as the norm for advancement and perpetuate this corrosive style. Regardless, the reservoir of leadership talent is depleted with palpable and extended institutional consequences.

The president is the guardian of the institution's vision. There is a direct correlation between his/her authentic advocacy of the goals and the level of enthusiasm and commitment among the university community. Therefore, the communication of the collective sense of the future is fundamental to the institution's success, the president's success, and the continuing recruitment of aspiring, developing leaders. The communication must be consistent, multidimensional, and democratic. The message is widely disseminated in various forms. It is not confined to a particular event, time of year, or constituency. The essential elements of the message should be woven into the ubiquitous "elevator" speech, academic community forums, commencement addresses, and donor recognition events. Many rising stars will make a personal connection to the institution and its future based on the quality and consistency of the aspiration as codified in the mission/vision values, and in their trust of the messengers. Future leaders can be attracted to an institution not by rankings or assumed reputations, but by the promise of personal and institutional relevance and fulfillment exemplified by what is said, who says it, and the perceived degree of avid acceptance by university leadership and community alike.

Attitudes

Attitude is a life force in any enterprise, including the university. Positive, collaborative attitudes among the leadership team can transform a challenge into an opportunity. When optimism, rooted in full understanding of the situation, becomes an institution-wide habit, the options for resolving the serious issues proliferate. It is one of the key elements in the institution's culture, and it is markedly influenced by the president and the senior leadership team. A pervasive, "can-do together" attitude can be a potent antidote for persistent, change-resistant silos and back-bench cynicism. As goals are realized, the sense of optimism is affirmed and becomes attractive to those still reserving judgment about whether to come aboard. When the inevitable difficulties and obstacles arise, attitude is a valued ally in problem-solving and on-campus cohesion. It can assist in aggregating both leadership and faculty and staff to assess and then actively support a pathway to resolving the problem.

But the popular, active adoption of such a supportive and congruent attitude is based in the leadership, in the veracity of the leadership team's consistent and multifaceted communication, and in their personal, transparent mode of connecting with the university community. Good news or not so good, the leader's habit of sharing what is happening and the routes to resolution confirms his/her perceived effectiveness and reinforces confidence across the institution's constituencies as well as community-building, integrative attitudes throughout the institution.

Some lessons learned across an extended career in higher education remain indelible, and perhaps more vital now than when first discovered. For example, local philosopher leaders have inspired those around them by living the values they embraced for a lifetime, and in the process, changed their communities, their institutions as well as individual behaviors. They are the culture shapers and mentors who offer lessons in lives well lived based on mission, vision, and values.

One of these unacknowledged heroes spoke of "leaving the woodpile higher than you found it." This metaphor produced faint resonance among most urban dwellers. But for those who have spent a winter with wood-fired heating, the message is personal and verifiable.

This declaration is relevant and meaningful especially to university leaders. The university and its focus on student success and serving the community, region, or state as "stewards of place" traverses the tenure of any individual regardless of title or responsibility. College and university leaders have a rooted responsibility to advancing the culture of learning, leading, and serving during their tenure in such servant–leadership roles. The "woodpile" is not confined to the size of the endowment, the number of new buildings, or the prowess of the athletic teams. It is also the firm seeding of leadership talent recruitment and development as a perpetual role and a valued responsibility.

Leaders should begin their service with the clear awareness of this duty that transcends their personal advancement or success. Leaders build the future now in the choices made about values, style, team members, and the shaping of institutional culture.

Central to fulfilling the fullest expression of one's leadership role is intentionally identifying, recruiting, and cultivating talent for the leadership pipeline. If done effectively, the influence will last well beyond the leader's term of service. And those who are not currently serving at the institution, and who may never know the leader's name, will be immeasurably enriched by pathways and styles purposely selected as vital to the institution's culture. The university's "woodpile" will be replenished well into the future by a succession of effective leaders who embrace these unique, service-focused roles.

Recommended Readings

Bennis, W., Goleman, D., & O'Toole, J. (2008). *Transparency: How Leaders Create a Culture of Cando.* San Francisco: Jossey-Bass Publishers.

Heifetz, R., & Linsky, M. (2002). *Leadership on the Line.* Boston: Harvard College.

Kouzes, J.M., & Posner, B. (2011). *Credibility, How Leaders Gain and Lose It, Why People Demand It.* San Francisco: Jossey-Bass Publishers.

Kouzes, J.M., & Posner, B. (2012). *The Leadership Challenge.* San Francisco: Jossey-Bass Publishers.

Ron, H. (1994). *Leadership With No Easy Answers.* Boston: Harvard College.

Shaw, R.B. (1997). *Trust in the Balance.* San Francisco: Jossey-Bass Publishers.

Useem, M. (1998). *The Leadership Moment.* New York City: Three Rivers Press.

CHAPTER 11

Managing Diversity as a University Strategy

Geetha Garib

Introduction

Universities often have staff members originating from all around the world, as academics tend to have global mindsets and academic specializations often cross-national borders. However, diversity can be found everywhere in any university as there are different departments, studies, students, and often staff members. How this diversity is being handled within universities can make a huge difference for the ranking of universities, as universities can greatly profit from the diversity they have to offer. Specifically, diversity in universities can create unique international networks in academic fields, whereby they can outperform other universities. Furthermore, when diversity is fully integrated in a university, students from all around the world are attracted to such a university, whereby diversity is increased, and therefore becomes a value-added asset. Thus, this chapter is of great relevance for universities who want to manage the present diversity, small or large, in their university and benefit from this diversity. In addition, if a university wants to use diversity as a university strategy in order to reach outstanding teaching and excellent research capabilities, this chapter will provide guidelines on how to set up such a strategy.

Universities that are ranked as the best universities in the world typically have staff members originating from all around the world. Dealing with diverse staff members may mean that you will need to deal with different cultures. However, diversity at universities can also be caused by gender and race.

In this chapter, the main diversity elements at universities are discussed. Consequently, two models explaining how to implement diversity are discussed. These models can be used as main guidelines when considering the management of diversity as a university strategy to reach outstanding teaching and excellent research capabilities.

Diversity Elements at Universities: Gender, Race, and Culture

The main diversity elements found at universities are gender, age, race, and culture. While at universities in most developed countries the male–female ratio of students is very evenly balanced, the female–male ratio of university teachers is often not well balanced. Most universities still have more male teachers than female teachers. On a higher management level, we find that the majority of school heads, deans and university presidents are male. Concerning race, most universities still have far more Caucasian university teachers than non-Caucasian university teachers. Even though, the origin of this finding may be linked to the fact that university students in general are also more of Caucasian origin, we still do not find an equal and well-balanced representation of university staff members for most universities. Furthermore, as academic scholars often need to cross borders in order to find other academic scholars with similar interests, most universities prefer to recruit staff members of the same nationality of the country where the university is based. An HR university department may explain this fact by the extra expenses linked to relocation costs. Often, only rich and well-known universities are able to attract academics from abroad for exactly this financial reason. However, in this way famous and rich universities will provide in their own sustainability while unknown and poor universities will not be able to flourish. Diversity can actually make a difference for universities, but the university management needs to see the value of diversity for their university.

The three diversity elements can be referred to as gender diversity, racial diversity, and cultural diversity. In universities, the representation of staff members should include each of these diversity types in order to make use of diversity in an advantageous manner.

Implementation Practices: Two Models

There are several existing models of diversity management. However, none of these models have actually been remodeled to be implemented in a university setting. In this chapter, the model of Ely and Thomas (2001) based on three main perspectives of diversity is explained and elaborated. Furthermore, the model based on a diversity-based organizational identity developed by Rink and Ellemers (2007) is mentioned (Table 11.1).

Model 1: Diversity Perspectives

Universities can have three major implementation practices based on three diversity perspectives developed by Ely and Thomas (2001). Ely and Thomas (2001) have distinguished three main perspectives on diversity.

The first perspective is called the discrimination-and-fairness perspective. According to this perspective, diversity is considered as a "moral imperative to ensure justice and fair treatment of all members of society" (Ely & Thomas, 2001). The value for diversity is low, and it is used only as an argument of why they do not discriminate. There is a limited connection between diversity and work. An indicator of progress for organizations following this perspective takes place when there is an increased amount of diversity, even in invisible or irrelevant positions. Universities who follow this diversity perspective have almost no or only a handful of non-Caucasian/female/young/non-national full researchers and university teachers. If they do appoint under-represented group members in their faculty, they will most likely aim to do this on a temporary basis or for courses that

Table 11.1 Models for Diversity Strategy in Universities

Model 1: Diversity perspectives by Ely and Thomas (2001)	1. Discrimination-and-fairness perspective: low value for diversity
	2. Access-and-legitimacy perspective: moderate value for diversity
	3. Integration-and-learning perspective: high value for diversity
Model 2: Diversity-based organizational identity by Rink and Ellemers (2007)	1. Trust
	2. Time
	3. Feeling of togetherness

demand extra time and effort. Deans, heads of schools, and full professors are all male, Caucasian, and citizens of the nationality where the university is based.

The second perspective is called the access-and-legitimacy perspective. This perspective is based on the idea that diversity is not a core element of the organization, but diversity is only marginally active as diversity is only used as a means to access specific markets and legitimize the representation of their staff diversity. Diversity is moderately valued, and merely an indirect connection between diversity and work takes place. An indicator of progress of organizations following this perspective is when they have an increased amount of diversity in boundary or visible positions. Universities who follow this diversity perspective have some (i.e., less than 30–50%) non-Caucasian/female/young/non-national full researchers and university teachers. They do appoint some of these under-represented group members in their faculty, but are more likely not to give these staff members tenure or try to let them work harder than non-diversity members. A qualified person of a minority group needs to show a lot of extra talent and experience than a similarly qualified majority group member in order to get appointed at university. A university would perhaps appoint several full professors from diversity groups. However, deans, heads of schools, and full professors are still mostly male, Caucasian, and citizens of the nationality where the university is based.

The third perspective is called the integration-and-learning perspective. According to this perspective, diversity is used as way to perform and innovate work in organizations. Diversity is strongly valued, and is considered a main asset of the organization. There is a clear direct connection between diversity and work as it is completely integrated in work processes. Furthermore, an indicator of progress for organizations following this perspective is when diversity is visible in top positions of people who are in charge of the organization, and when there is a shared value among staff members that diversity is a resource for learning. Unfortunately, universities who follow this perspective are rare. Universities who follow this diversity perspective have a good and healthy representation (i.e., about 30–50%) of non-Caucasian/female/young/non-national full researchers and university teachers. University directors appoint quite some of these under-represented group members in their faculty, and will provide tenure positions to diversity members. A qualified person of a minority group needs to show an equal amount of talent and experience as a similarly qualified majority group member in order to get appointed at this university. A university would appoint several full professors from diversity groups. In some cases, deans, heads of schools, and full professors can be female/from a different nationality. For example, since 2007 Harvard has its first female president. Thus, world-leading universities may set an example to other universities of which diversity perspective may be the best for universities who would like to show excellent performance.

Model 2: Management of Diversity Based on Creating a Diversity Identity

Next to the implementation practice of diversity at universities, the management of a university needs to think about how to achieve benefits of diversity, while reducing the risks of diversity. Benefits of diversity are creating more innovation (Sastre, 2015), an increased productivity (Gonzalez & Denisi, 2009), and being able to fulfill a wider range of tasks (Northcroft et al., 1995). Risks of diversity can consist of low commitment (Jehn et al., 1999) and task conflict (Pelled et al., 1999). In order to manage diversity in such a way to create benefits, one needs to take into account some main principles: time, trust, and togetherness. These elements are needed to create a diversity identity.

Rink and Ellemers (2007) developed a model with a diversity-based organizational identity. According to Rink and Ellemers (2007), "differences among team members in organizations are congruent with norms and expectations, diversity can become a basis for organizational identifications." They stress the importance of creating a common and higher goal for all members in an organization, especially for diverse members. In this way, members may be diverse, but they all have something in common: the goal of their organization. Thus, in a university the goal may be to create excellent teaching modules and publish outstanding research for all university staff members. In order to reach the latter goal, they may actually need diversity as it can create excellence and therefore, enable them to reach the goal. As a consequence, diversity may become a key element for their identity as it will motivate them to reach a higher goal.

However, in order to reach this diversity-based identity, they will need time, trust, and a feeling of togetherness.

It will take time before diverse members in an organization get to know each other. Therefore, one needs to take into account the time element when expecting positive outcomes of benefits. It has been found that heterogeneous team members are more able to produce innovation and productivity compared with homogeneous teams when taking into account the time element (Earley & Mosakowski, 2000; Harrison et al., 1998; Schippers et al., 2003; Watson et al., 1993).

Furthermore, time may be needed to create trust among diverse members. As members trust each other, they are more loyal to each other and are more committed to what they all want to achieve. Trust is also needed in order to create transparency and space for communication. Only in a trusting atmosphere, open communication is possible, and finally a feeling of togetherness can be the result.

Thirdly, a feeling of togetherness can be created both by trust, over time, and by open communication. As diversity often implies the existence of a majority and a minority group, the in-group bias can act as a threat to the shared commitment and identification among members (Tajfel & Turner, 1986). According to social identity theory, the in-group bias appears among majority members who consider out-group/minority members as a threat in their organization. Therefore, they will give a preference to other majority members compared with minority members in the organization. For example, in a university, the majority of staff members in an economics department may be male, as there are 18 male university teachers and 2 female university teachers. In this case, when the department needs to democratically choose a new departmental head, the male university teachers may prefer to have a male departmental head as they identify more with men than with women. Therefore, the feeling of togetherness is not very strong among all members of the department as the in-group bias inhibits this feeling. In sum, to ensure a suitable management of diversity at universities, one needs to take into account also the elements of time, trust, and togetherness.

Conclusion

This chapter is aimed to create awareness for managers of universities that the quality of teaching and research can be strongly influenced by the diversity of university staff members. In order to deal with diversity at universities, a strategy needs to be employed in such a way so that benefits of diversity can flourish while the risks are mitigated. Figure 11.1 highlights the process for deciding diversity strategy for universities.

As shown in Figure 11.1, the management of diversity should be aimed at identifying which type of diversity needs to focused on. Secondly, a specific perspective on diversity needs to be chosen. Thirdly, the management of diversity needs the presence of a university culture in which time, trust, open communication, and a reduced in-group bias are leading to a diversity-based identity. If these steps are taken, universities can use diversity as a way to fulfill their organizational strategy and lead to excellence in their research and teaching capabilities.

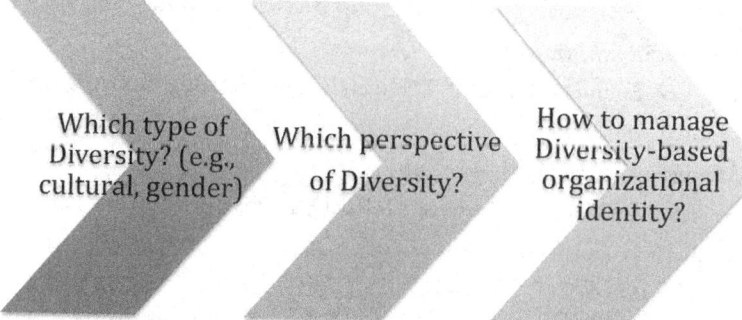

Figure 11.1 Process for deciding diversity strategy for universities.

References

Earley. O.C., & Mosakowski, E. (2000).Creating hybrid team cultures: An empirical test of transnational team functioning. *Academy of Management Journal, 43*, 26–49.

Ely, R.J., & Thomas, D.A. (2001). Cultural diversity at work: The effects of diversity perspectives on work group processes and outcomes. *Administrative Science Quarterly, 46*(2), 229–273.

Gonzalez, J.A., & Denisi, A.S. (2009). Cross-level effects of demography and diversity climate on organizational attachment and firm effectiveness. *Journal of Organizational Behavior, 30*, 21–40.

Harrison, D.A., Price, K.H., & Bell, M.P. (1998). Beyond relational demography: Time and the effects of surface- and deep-level diversity on work group cohesion. *Academy of Management Journal, 41*, 96–107.

Jehn, K.A., Northcroft, G.B., & Neale, M.A. (1999). Why differences make a difference: A field study of diversity, conflict and performance in workgroups. *Administrative Science Quarterly, 44*, 741–763.

Northcroft, G.B., Polzer, J.T., Neale, M., & Kramer, R.S. (1995). Diversity, social identity, and performance: Emergent social dynamics in cross-functional teams. In S.E. Jackson & M.N. Ruderman (Eds.), *Diversity in Work Teams: Research Paradigms for a Changing Workplace* (pp. 69–96). Washington, DC: American Psychological Association.

Pelled, L.H., Eisenhardt, K.M., & Xin, K.R. (1999). Exploring the black box: An analysis of work group diversity, conflict, and performance. *Administrative Science Quarterly, 11*, 1–28.

Rink, F., & Ellemers, N. (2007). Diversity as a basis for shared organizational identity: The norm congruity principle. *British Journal of Management, 18* (1), 17–27.

Sastre, J.F. (2015). The impact of R&D teams' gender diversity on innovation outputs. *International Journal of Entrepreneurship and Small Business, 24*(1), 142–162.

Schippers, M.C., Den Hartog, D.N., Koopman, P.L., & Wienk, J.A. (2003). Reflexivity and diversity in teams: The moderating effects of outcome interdependence and group longevity. *Journal of Organizational Behavior, 24*, 729–802.

Tajfel, H., & Turner, J.C. (1986). The social identity theory of intergroup behavior. In S. Worchel & W.G. Austin (Eds.), *Psychology of Intergroup Relations* (pp. 7–24). Chicago: Nelson-Hall Publishers.

Watson, W.E., Kumar, K., & Michaelsen, L.K. (1993). Cultural diversity's impact on interaction processes and performance: Comparing homogeneous and diverse task groups. *Academy of Management Journal, 36*, 590–602.

CHAPTER 12

Managing Duty of Care Obligations in a University Setting

Lisbeth Claus

With globalization, the legal and moral duty of care obligations of employers for the health, safety, and security of their traveling employees have developed as a cornerstone of any human capital risk management strategy. Although universities are increasingly becoming aware of the duty of care obligations to their students, faculty, administration, and staff traveling internationally on university business, they lag other sectors and industries in implementing duty of care strategies and tactics. The purpose of this chapter is to focus on the nature of the duty of care obligations of U.S. universities, identify common mistakes universities make in managing (or failing to manage) duty of care, and suggest some leading practices to assist universities in implementing and sustaining a robust duty of care program.

With the globalization of education, there is increased international travel of various constituencies (i.e.., students, faculty, administration, and staff) on behalf of the university. The global dimension of student learning has become an integral part of the modern educational experience with students participating in study abroad programs, engaging in service-learning activities around the world, competing in athletic events, participating in cultural exchanges, and taking faculty-led international trips for credit. These international educational and living abroad activities take place away from the university's campus. They are happening in an unfamiliar environment for the student beyond the controlled space of the classroom or campus of the partnering university. Faculty employed at U.S. colleges and universities are also traveling frequently abroad to engage in research, teaching, and professional service activities. They may be leading groups of student on trips for course credit, attend international academic conferences to present papers, pursue sabbaticals in other countries, engage in field research abroad, and share their academic expertise as a service to other countries as part of international exchanges and in response to crises (e.g., natural disasters, pandemics, etc.). University administration and staff often travel abroad for international recruiting purposes, establishing partnerships with other schools and for fundraising. In some instances, U.S. universities have established branch campuses in other countries with local and expatriate faculty, administration, and staff. As a result of these developments, international travel as part of one's education or work entails many risks to the university in terms of the health, safety, and security of these travelers.

Universities have a legal and moral obligation to mitigate "foreseeable" risk when their students and employees travel abroad on university business. This obligation is known as duty of care. The legal notion of "duty of care" implies that individuals and organizations have legal obligations to act toward others and the public in a prudent and cautious manner to avoid the risk of "reasonable foreseeable" injury. Employers have a duty of care obligation for the health, safety, security, and well-being of their employees as they fulfill their work obligations and for their customers who use their products or services (Claus & Yost, 2010). Duty of care is a relatively new dimension of university management that is receiving increased attention—although not to the same extent as other university issues related to campus violence, sexual harassment, bullying, or student health behavior.

In a 2011 Global Benchmarking Study on duty of care, the scholastic sector ranked worst among all industries and sectors in assuming its duty of care obligations (Claus, 2011). Several reasons can be put forth for this lack of attention such as a general lack of duty of care obligation awareness, the fact that students are not employees, the independent nature of faculty, the growing budget constraints of many educational institutions, and the eroding business model of brick and mortar higher education. However, increasingly, universities are involved in litigation for failure to protect their students and faculty when traveling abroad on their behalf (*Boisson v. Arizona board of Regents et al.*, 2015). This is not only costly for universities but also affects their reputational risk and, ultimately, their ability to attract and recruit students, donations, and funding. In the past few years, duty of care has slowly appeared on the radar screen of university administrators. This is often the case after hearing about a devastating incident involving a student or faculty member abroad. While some universities have taken proactive steps, many have not. Most universities probably fall somewhere in between, meaning that they know there are risks, but they think that it will not happen to them or simply do not have the knowhow to take concerted action to address their duty of care obligations.

The purpose of this chapter is to focus on the nature of the duty of care obligations of U.S. universities, identify common mistakes that universities make in duty of care management, and suggest leading practices to assist universities in implementing and sustaining a robust duty of care program.

The Legal Framework of Duty of Care Obligations at U.S. Universities

Universities are complex organizations. Not only do they have different internal and external constituencies—some of which are employees such as faculty, staff, administrators, and others who are students with whom they have a special relationship. There is no *per se* general duty of care legislation in the United States, but employees can seek damages for negligence on the part of the employer for failing to take adequate measures to protect them from reasonably foreseeable risks. This applies when employees travel abroad on behalf of their employer. Four elements generally comprise a traditional negligence cause of action: (1) a *duty* of care obligation that requires the employer to conform to a certain standard of conduct; (2) a *breach* of that duty or a failure of the employer to conform to the standard; (3) a factual and proximate cause or reasonably close connection between the injury and the breach; and (4) an injury resulting from that breach. All must coexist to claim negligence (Owen, 2007). The legal standard for establishing a duty of care obligation is, however, different for students than faculty, staff, and administrators because students are not employees of the university.

A number of legal scholars (Griffin, 2007; Rhim, 1996; Yeo, 2002; Zamastil, 2008) have reviewed the legal doctrines applicable to university duty of care of students. The conclusions that they derived from the case reviews is presented here at a summary level. Three major legal theories have evolved over time. First, it was common to use the *in loco parentis* (in lieu of a parent) doctrine. The university was considered a parent and had a certain authority to regulate the conduct of their students in place of the parents, resulting in a university duty of care obligations to protect their students from foreseeable harm. As a result, they had the authority to impose certain regulations on student conduct. The use of this doctrine changed in the 1950s and 1960s (e.g., during political campus demonstrations) as students were deemed to be adults (and not children) who are accountable for their own actions. Note that this doctrine is, however, still commonly applied to high school students. A second legal framework that invokes university duty of care for student is the *landowner-invitee* theory. The student is an invitee who enters onto the property of the school at the express or implied invitation of the property owner (i.e., the university). As a result, universities have a duty of care obligation toward their students and must prevent on-campus harms and injuries while students are on their premise. This theory is less applicable for off-campus activities. The third legal theory is that there is a special relationship between universities and students, which gives rise to reasonable duty of care to protect students from harm. This is, obviously, the case when students travel off-campus for school-related activities that are sponsored by the educational institution. This has been extensively documented for student athletics (Miyamoto, 1988; Rhim, 1996). Similarly this applies for off-campus activities related to university-organized trips (e.g., faculty-led student trips for credit). In *Boisson v. Arizona Board of Regents et al.* (2015), the court identified seven factors to determine whether an off-campus activity is a school activity that gives rise to duty of care: (1) the purpose of the activity; (2) whether the activity was part of the course curriculum; (3) whether the school had supervisory authority over the activity; (4) whether the risk existed independent of the school involvement; (5) whether the activity was voluntary; (6) whether a school employee was present during the activity, or should have been; and (7) whether the activity involved a dangerous project initiated on-campus but built off-campus.

The special university–student relationship can also be invoked even when students study at an educational partner institution (i.e., study abroad programs). The agreements that university enter into with educational partners constitute an agency relationship with such institutions.

Hence, the university must ensure that the partners meet acceptable duty of care standards for these exchange students.

In the case of university employees, generally the staff and the administration are "at will" while faculty are usually on contract working on behalf of the institution. The U.S. legal framework for employer duty of care is not as clear cut as in other countries (especially Canada, Europe, Australia, and New Zealand). Employers have overall responsibility for health, safety, and security of their employees under OSHA, the Occupational Safety and Health Act (1970). Workers Compensation, a federally mandated benefit administered on a state-by-state basis, is an insurance that provides wage replacement and medical benefits to employees injured while working. OSHA and Workers Compensation are not extra-territorial, meaning that they do not extend beyond their boundaries. Yet, there is no doubt that a special relationship exists between the university and the faculty, staff and administration that it applies even when they are abroad. This creates under the common law concept of (torts) a special duty of care obligation on behalf of the university for the health, safety, and security of these employees whether they are "at will" or on contract and, independently whether they work on- or off-campus. Failing to assume this responsibility can lead to a claim of negligence.

Having established a legal obligation for duty of care of the university for both students and employees, the corner stone of any duty of care responsibility is for the educational institution to mitigate foreseeable risk when employees (and board of trustee members) travel for study or work purposes on behalf of the university.

Shortcomings of Universities with Regard to Duty of Care

Educational institutions overall have extremely poor duty of care performance. Key research findings comparing the scholastic sector to other sectors (government and nonprofit organizations) and industries (Claus, 2011; Claus & Giordano, 2013) indicate that educational institutions and their decision makers have lower risk perceptions, awareness, and ratings on all duty of care practices in each step of the duty of care integrated risk management model and have the lowest duty of care overall baseline (see Figure 12.1).

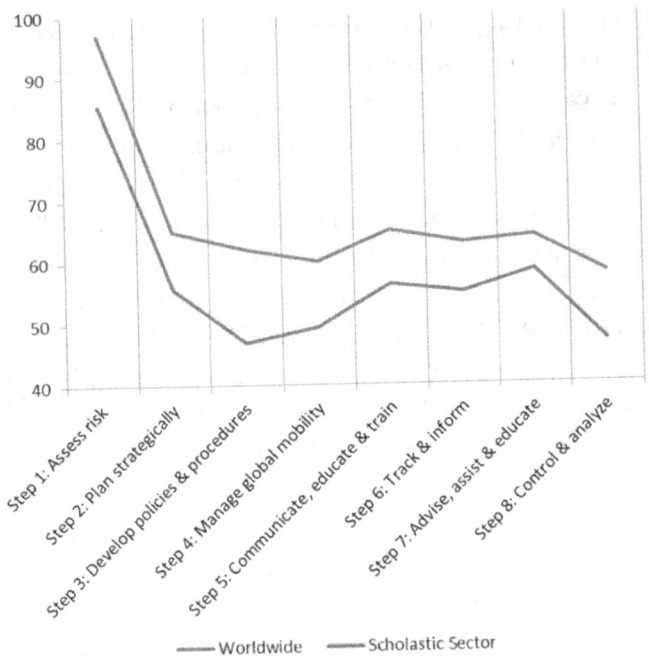

Figure 12.1 Scholastic sector duty of care baseline versus worldwide global benchmarking study (2011).

When it comes to managing duty of care in a university setting, educational institutions—although well-intentioned—often tend to make a number of mistakes that are not in line with the leading practices that the corporate sector is adopting.

Mistake #1: Focusing Duty of Care Attention on Students While Neglecting Faculty and Staff

The focus of U.S. universities in recent years has been on campus safety. Managing duty of care is still not on the radar screen for most educational institutions. Educational facilities are increasingly focusing on student risk (both on campus and for student trips led by faculty), but they still tend to overlook the risk associated with international travel of their employees (i.e., faculty, staff, and administration). Yet, for the most part, they endorse such travel through funding (e.g., conference attendance and sabbaticals of faculty). Even universities that are leading in terms of managing duty of care report that it is a lot easier to focus their duty of care efforts on students than on faculty. Universities must deal with a highly governance driven and independent faculty, who often decide to play by their own rules and prefer to make independent decisions (Claus, 2014). Universities must increase their duty of care awareness and knowledge at the administrative level and broaden general awareness of its importance throughout the university community. They must focus on all constituencies (students, faculty, staff, and administration) in duty of care and elevate duty of care to the same level of importance as other complex, yet conventional, behavioral health, and safety risk management issues including sexual harassment, bullying, drug/alcohol use, mental illness, and campus violence.

Mistake #2: Relying on Insurance as a Substitute for Duty of Care

University administrators rely heavily on insurance for all types of risks that students and faculty may encounter on- and off-campus. While insurance (especially health coverage while abroad) is absolutely prudent and necessary, it is not sufficient in assuming one's duty of care obligations. Universities must go beyond insurance and mitigate all types of duty of care risk. In order to do so, they must identify the university-specific travel risks and vulnerabilities that they have and review the possible gaps and overlaps in their insurance coverage. Many insurance policies do not have an evacuation rider, nor coverage for leisure travel—often taken at the front or back end of a sabbatical or study abroad program—nor a mental illness rider. In reviewing their insurance coverage, university administrators must consider the adequacy of the minimum standard provisions that are required by law without which it would be reckless to operate any education abroad activity (Braun & Gemmeke, 2005).

Mistake #3: Not Having a Formal Organizational Structure to Deal with Duty of Care

While all organizations must deal with a lack of duty of care awareness among stakeholders, universities seem to have difficulty mobilizing and coordinating the different stakeholders involved in duty of care implementation. Educational institutions are often structured with a dual line of authority, namely an administrative and academic line, making implementation of any change in policies and procedures much more difficult. In addition, many higher educational institutions routinely do not have an integrated policy on safety, security, and crisis management (Helsloot & Jong, 2006). Somewhere within the university, there must be a formal structure to manage duty of care. When starting to implement duty of care, university administrators usually begin by setting up a university-wide duty of care task force with representatives from all campus stakeholders to identify the university's vulnerabilities. This is a great first step but should be followed by setting up separate, yet interrelated, strategic, and tactical duty of care teams and appointing key university decision makers (ranging from safety, security, risk management, campus health, HR, travel, university operations, deans, and department heads) with well-defined roles and responsibilities.

Mistake #4: Failing to Develop a Robust Duty of Care Risk Mitigation Plan

Universities have developed campus safety and health plans to respond to various campus incidents that can threaten the health, safety, and security of students, faculty, and staff. These have often been developed a response to campus violence, the rising incidence of behavioral health issues among students and recent epidemics such as H1N1 flue, SARS, and Ebola. But, when it comes to mitigating off-campus risk, universities tend to lag behind in developing a robust duty of care risk mitigation plan. Although travel risk may differ from one educational institution to another, each university must develop a risk mitigation plan for the risks and threats that their students and faculty face while traveling for specific purposes and locations. The strategic duty of care plan (and team) focuses on developing risk mitigation plans and ensuring appropriate policies and procedures are in place while the tactical duty care plan (and incident management team) is responsible for the development of incident management protocols. Both strategic and tactical duty of care plans once implemented must be updated regularly based on changing circumstances, lessons learned, and best practices shared.

Mistake #5: Having Vague or No Travel Authorization Policies

While universities often have boiler plate policies for university travel and reimbursement, they often fall short of including travel authorizations that restrict travel to high-risk locations. A good example was during the 2014 Ebola crisis. The university's travel management policies and procedures were inadequate to deal with students and faculty volunteers wanting to travel to the affected African countries for learning and service purposes in spite of imposed travel bans. U.S. universities had a wide range of responses ranging from prohibiting university-sponsored travel for faculty and students, banning travel with the exception of Ebola-related research and relief work that did not include direct patient contact, banning travel expect for care and assistance providers on a humanitarian mission, allowing travel on their own under the auspices of other agencies, discouraging travel, to having no Ebola-related travel policies at all (Péres-Peńa, 2014). In each case, universities had to balance the service mission of their institutions with the protection of their employees. While the Ebola may be viewed as an unusual case for concern, students and faculty commonly travel to countries with high or extreme health and security risk whether for study or research and their universities have no or limited travel authorization processes in place.

Mistake #6: Failing to Assess Health, Safety, and Security Risk Prior to Departure

One of the basic legal requirements by which employers mitigate "foreseeable" risk is by initially assessing the risk. Travel risk assessment for university-related travel, therefore, requires the university to assess the health, safety, and security risks prior to any planned trip for all travellers whether students, faculty, or staff. In doing so, they must use legitimate and reliable risk assessment sources ranging from U.S. State Department sites to the assistance of specialized risk analysis providers. The failure of universities to conduct risk assessment prior to travel, have medical and security risk level alerts in place, and make travel authorizations based on reliable risk assessment makes them extremely vulnerable. A particular risk that is often overlooked is the mental health of students and their ability to cope with an adjustment to a foreign country often leading to repatriation and evacuation of students prior to the end of their scheduled study abroad program (Quigley et al., 2015).

Mistake #7: Inadequately Preparing Students, Faculty, and Staff for International Travel

While many universities have extensive cultural, educational, and other preparation for study abroad and faculty-led international programs, they rarely include duty of care education and training. Duty of care preparation includes communicating the extent of the risk of the country under consideration, prescribing preventive courses of action to mitigate risk, educating students and faculty on restrictive behaviors while abroad, and ensuring that they are prepared to deal with different potential risk scenarios. Even low-risk countries can be potentially dangerous as travellers find themselves in unfamiliar environments. Real-time risk data based on the university's travel risk profile can provide opportunities for teachable moments with faculty and students. This allows the university to proactively intervene with a customized just-in-time online-delivered intervention.

Mistake #8: Ignoring Where Their Travellers Are at All Times

In order to be able to assist students and faculty when studying or working abroad, universities must be able to identify where their travellers are located at all times. Yet, most universities do not have the capability to track traveling students and faculty. Hence, in case of a natural disaster (e.g., earthquake, tsunami, etc.), human-made disaster (e.g., political unrest, terrorist attack, war, etc.), or personal emergency incidents (e.g., road accidents and illness), they are not in a position to assist their students and faculty and/or evacuate them when needed. Only when they are able to locate and communicate with their traveling students and employees can universities advise them what to do. In addition to tracking their travellers, universities are also starting to implement emergency response notification systems and engaging reliable assistance providers for dealing with the medical and security incidents of their traveling faculty, staff, and students.

Mistake #9: Failing to Enforce Their Travel Management Policies and Procedures

Many organizations often fail to ensure compliance their travel policies and procedures and universities are no exception. Even with the best duty of care plans, policies and procedures in place, unless universities can create a reciprocal duty of loyalty from their faculty and students, their risk management efforts will not be successful. In a true duty of care culture, students and faculty do not compete with the interests of the university but follow the policies and procedures that have been designed to mitigate travel risk and protect them from harm to the extent possible. This includes, among others, the use of approved travel vendors, obtaining travel authorization, ensuring that travellers have completed required training prior to departure and linking faculty travel reimbursement to compliance.

Mistake #10: Poorly Managing Their Reputational Risk When Incidents Occur

A final mistake that universities make is that they often lack a coordinated internal and external response to duty of care incidents involving their students or faculty. Unless they have an incident and crisis management plan (and team) in place and good coordination with their assistance providers, the internal coordination of their activities and decision making is often jeopardized and may they set themselves up for law suits by the way they handle an incident. Universities must also properly deal with these incidents externally with the public at large and manage their reputational risk. Unless a university public relations spokesperson is a member of the duty of care incident management team, miscommunication often occurs. In case of duty of care incidents, a certain amount of damage control may be required to "stay on top" of social media related to the incident as its usage is very much part of the university community and often the source of misleading data.

Leading Duty of Care Practice for University Management

Even with the best planning and risk mitigation mechanisms, things do happen and no one can fully prevent the various health, safety, and security threats that are out there. Yet, duty of care best practices inform employers of standards of practice to which they are expected to be held by their internal and external stakeholders. Operating at a standard also helps fend off duty of care negligence lawsuits that are increasingly common in the nonprofit scholastic sector.

Specific best practices for university administrators to implement regarding duty of care management have been proposed overall as well as for universities that are still new to duty of care (Claus, 2014; Claus & Yost, 2013). These best practices follow the steps of the duty of care integrated risk management model (Claus & Giordano, 2013). In Figure 12.2, a number of leading practices and specific action steps are suggested for managing the duty of care shortcoming identified in the university setting.

1. Increase duty of care awareness and knowhow at the administrative level
   - Focus on all constituencies (students, faculty, staff, and administration) in duty of care
   - Elevate duty of care to the same level of importance as sexual harassment, bullying, and campus violence
2. Go beyond insurance and manage duty of care risk
   - Review your insurance coverage for gaps and overlaps
   - Identify your university-specific threats and vulnerabilities regarding duty of care
3. Design a formal structure within the university to manage duty of care
   - Set up a university-wide duty of care task force
   - Appoint a duty of care strategic planning team
   - Appoint an incident management team
4. Develop an overall duty of care risk management plan
   - Develop a risk mitigation plan for different threats
   - Develop an incident management protocol
   - Update your plans regularly based on lessons learned
5. Implement travel management policies and procedures
   - Develop duty of care travel management policies and procedures for different university constituencies
   - Implement travel authorizations
6. Assess foreseeable risk prior to any planned trip for all travellers
   - Use legitimate risk assessment sources
   - Put medical and security risk level alerts in place

- Implement travel authorizations
- Screen students prior to study abroad programs

7. Communicate, educate, and train travellers about duty of care
   - Communicate risk prior to departure
   - Ensure that they are prepared to deal with different risk scenarios
   - Inform them of restricted and expected behaviors while abroad

8. Track and monitor traveling students, faculty, and staff
   - Assist and advise them of changing risk and what to do
   - Have reliable assistance providers for medical and security incidents
   - Implement an emergency response notification system for faculty, staff, and students

9. Ensure strict compliance with your policies and procedures
   - Enforce travel authorizations
   - Ensure that travelers have completed required training prior to departure
   - Link travel reimbursement to faculty compliance

10. Manage your reputational risk
    - Make university PR a member of the duty of care incident management team

Figure 12.2 Leading duty of care practices and action steps for university management.

Conclusions

It is unfortunate that many universities are still not aware of the risks associated with the travel of students, faculty, and staff under their auspices. It often takes an incident or law suit in the educational sector to raise awareness of their moral and legal duty of care obligations. Yet, even when are aware of the need to mitigate these risks, they—often unknowingly—make mistakes. This chapter discussed the legal obligations of U.S. universities to mitigate travel risk, identified common mistakes universities make in managing duty of care, and suggested some leading practices to assist universities in implementing and sustaining a robust duty of care program. It is ironic that institutions that are charged with the education of others often fail to educate themselves in regard to their duty of care obligations.

References

Boisson v. Arizona Board of Regents et al. (2015). No.1 CA-CV 13-0588, 3-10-2105.

Braun, H., & Gemmeke, J. (2005). Beyond duty: Insurance management in education abroad programs. *International Educator, 2,* 52–55.

Claus, L. (2011). *Duty of Care and Travel Risk Management Global Benchmarking Study*. London, U.K.: AEA International Pte. Ltd.

Claus, L. (2014). *Duty of Care Scholastic Sector: Special Report*. London, England: International SOS.

Claus, L., & Giordano, E. (2013). Global employer duty of care: Protecting the health, safety, security and well-being of employees crossing borders. In L. Claus (Ed.), *Global HR Practitioner Handbook*, volume 1 (pp. 279–299). Silverton, OR: Global Immersion Press.

Claus, L. & Yost, R. (2010). A global view of university risk. *URMIA Journal*, August, 23–38.

Griffin, O.R. (2007). Confronting the evolving safety and security challenges at colleges and universities. *Pierce Law Review, 5*, 413–432.

Helsloot, I., & Jong, W. (2006). Risk management in higher education and research in the Netherlands. *Journal of Contingencies and Crisis Management, 3*, 142–159.

Miyamoto, T. (1988). Liability of colleges and universities for injuries during extracurricular activities. *Journal of College and University Law, 2*, 19–176.

Occupational Safety and Health Act. (1970). Public Law 91-596.

Owen, D.G. (2007). The five elements of negligence. *Hofstra Law Review, 4*, 1671–1686.

Péres-Peña, R. (2014). Universities are prodded to tighten travel rules. *The New York Times*, October 22, A7.

Quigley, R., Claus, L., & Nixon, A. (2015). *Behavioral health morbidity for those studying or working internationally: A U.S. Exploratory Duty of Care Study*. Unpublished manuscript, Willamette University.

Rhim, A. (1996). The special relationship between student-athletes and colleges: An analysis of a heightened duty of care for the injury of students athletes. *Marquette Sports Law Review, 7*, 329–348.

Yeo, S. (2002). The responsibility of universities for their students' personal safety. *Southern Cross University Law Review, 6*, 77–105.

Zamastil, K. (2008). Universities' liabilities for negligence in study abroad programs: How they can protect their students and themselves. *Common Law Review, 39–44*.

CHAPTER 13

Conclusion

J. Mark Munoz and Neal King

Introduction

The global higher education landscape is filled with opportunities and challenges. On the one hand, thirst for skills and knowledge and technology, will continue to fill the seats (virtual and literal) in many institutions and will spur the delivery of education in innovative ways. On the other hand, there is intense competition, uneven market growth, and rapidly evolving paradigms that threaten the survival of bureaucratic and traditionally grounded institutions.

The cost of tertiary education is not affordable to everyone. In the United States, college tuition has risen about 1,200% in the past 35 years, with an average 4-year degree costing over $80,000 in tuition, room, board, and other expenses for residents studying in state universities (Cohen, 2014). U.S. students loaned about $1.1 trillion worth of debt, a figure higher than the country's credit card debts (Economist, 2014). Parents are seeking cheaper education options and are enrolling students in community colleges (Sanchez, 2014). This marks a fundamental shift in the social contract, where for generations investment in the next generation's education was seen as a collective responsibility—and investment—borne readily by taxpayers, this burden has shifted dramatically now to students and their families. This shift contributes to a growing class divide reflected by income disparity in the United States. Elite private schools continue to flourish and remain highly competitive; state-run and less robustly funded private institutions struggle for adequate resources. For-profit schools, after an early generation of largely unchallenged financial successes that were not always highly correlated with student success, are now being taken to task by the public and the federal government to provide a quality return on student investment in their programs of study. Universities will need to address diverse challenges such as quality and academic excellence, academic talent and workforce structure, commercial skills, change management and speed to market, and relationship with government (Ernst & Young, 2015). Emerging generations of "digital natives" learn, socialize, and process information differently than prior generations. They are likely more aligned with the society they will inhabit as adults than the professorate that seeks to prepare them for their roles in this society. The academy has to take responsibility to retrain and retool its instructors, curricula and pedagogies to anticipate, and meet and engage meaningfully with digital natives.

In essence, the contemporary education landscape requires "old school" institutions to embrace "new school" management philosophies— and core infrastructure—and execute dynamic strategic approaches.

Importance of Planning and Leading

The ability to manage institutions professionally and creatively will be critical to success. Attention to the management functions of planning and leading will be important.

Effective planning is essential. Carefully thinking through critical organizational goals is imperative. When planning, attention should be given to achieving high academic quality, accreditation, innovative instruction, technological adaptation, and internationalization. A well-developed Strategic Plan that incorporates the views of stakeholders will help define a successful future path.

Leadership in an institution will be the means in which important goals will be accomplished. Academic leaders need to build an effective management team, create a leadership pipeline ahead of time, and manage diversity as well as duty of care among its stakeholders. An institution's sustainability and profitability rest in the shoulders of its leaders. A well-developed leadership development plan can be a valuable tool for success.

Outlined below are some of the key learning points on planning and leading (Tables 13.1 and 13.2).

Table 13.1 Learning Points on Planning

Academic quality	Due attention needs to be provided on academic quality and rigor since it is a medium to maintain and build credibility and leads to sustainability. Planning and leadership is key, especially in consideration of matters resource allocation, mission alignment, and curriculum reform. This process should include the viewpoint of faculty and be focused toward the welfare of students and parents.
Accreditation	Accreditation contributes to the legitimacy of an institution, integrating accreditation expectations when setting goals is a step in the right direction. Visioning and planning needs to be realistic. Effective planning should bring together the future vision, strategic planning, enrollment plans, financial plans, human resource plans, and physical facilities plans. It should be anchored on the mission, driven by data, and inclusive of the views of key stakeholders. Periodic review is essential.
Strategic action model	Designing a proactive plan of action that anticipates needs and growth opportunities is essential. Factors that positively impact strategic action includes sound management practices, quality of leadership, alignment with market demand, organizational capacity, monitoring and review, and redirecting priorities.
Improvement of quality of instruction	Institutions must never rest on their laurels, the quest for instructional excellence should be a continuous process. Providing emphasis on student performance and pedagogical improvements leads to added value for the university.
Online methodologies	Given the relevance of online education in the technological as well as competitive context, consideration of its usage would prove valuable when developing plans. Considerations include educational enhancement potential, technology leveraging, cost factors, data gathering, and assessment.
Internationalization	Given that international markets offer opportunities to enhance the educational experience and increase enrollments, its inclusion in planning makes strategic sense. Comprehensive internationalization planning approach makes sense with due attention to structure and staffing, curriculum and cocurriculum learning outcomes, faculty and staff policies and practices, student mobility, and collaboration and partnerships.
Global higher education	When planning, taking on a global and holistic perspective with key emphasis on networking and strategic alliance formation can prove beneficial. In a globalized environment, institutions are well connected internationally. Linking with international networks can be tool toward enhancing educational quality as well as operational efficiency.

Table 13.2 Learning Points on Leading

Effective management team	An effective management team is the driving force behind successful leadership and should be craftfully and meticulously created. Team competency and professionalism, shared mission, and effective communication need to be considered.
Utilizing a leadership pipeline	Institutions run the risk of facing leadership vacuums, planning for a leadership pipeline well ahead of time makes strategic sense. A viable approach entails creating an environment with the right principles, attitudes, and practices in place with due consideration to shared mission and values, succession planning, continuity, maintained enthusiasm, and trust building.
Managing diversity	The composition of student body and workforce has changed considerable and will continue to change in the coming years; universities need to strive for leadership in managing diversity. This constitutes having the appropriate perspective and organizational identity with attention provided to type of diversity, perspective of diversity, and management of diversity-based organizational identity.
Managing duty of care	With challenges and pressures coming from all directions, it is easy for leaders to lose sight of priorities. Providing proper care and mitigating risks for its stakeholders should be a part of its overall mission. Managing duty of care requires that attention be placed on legal frameworks, shortcomings, and efficient leadership to ensure execution of plans.

The list provided above represents only a sliver of the numerous university management strategies outlined in the book. The findings suggest that (1) planning and leading operate in tandem—leaders create excellent plans in concert with their constituents, and well-developed plans make the implementation process easier for the leader and the institution; (2) planning in the university context requires the consideration of diverse factors; (3) a comprehensive and well-developed Strategic Plan would likely enhance the planning and leading process; (4) leadership in the university setting requires a dual ability to manage situations simultaneously using both a macro- and microperspective; leaders need to be able to think big, and act small; and (5) planning and leading needs to be aligned and recalibrated alongside a rapidly changing market environment; the practice is forever evolving with the times—there is no such thing as stasis.

Need for Self-Assessment

Findings in the book underscore the need to know one's organization well. An organizational Self-Assessment can help identify areas for improvement in Planning and Leading. Asking the right questions can make a difference. An example of helpful Self-Assessment questions is offered in Table 13.3.

Table 13.3 *Relevant Questions for Self-Assessment*

Planning	Has a Strategic Plan been developed? Did this plan incorporate the views and ideas of the institution's stakeholders? Are the plans in line with available resources? Do the plans consider market realities and competitive activities? Do the plans incorporate the best practices and challenge the institution to be the best it can be?
Leading	Are the leaders right for the institution at the current time? Do leaders motivate stakeholders to achieve excellence? Are leaders effective communicators who convey goals, direction, and policies clearly? Is a leadership development plan in place for current leaders and stakeholders? Is an appropriate performance feedback mechanism in place for leaders and stakeholders?

Taking on an inquisitive, efficiency-seeking management approach can lead to the identification of appropriate strategies.

A Future Path

The various chapters in this book highlight important attributes of the academic institutions of the 21st century:

Business-driven. More than ever, academic institutions need to consciously operate as a business, which they have always been, despite frequent distaste for this reality among faculty. While the delivery of top-rate education is paramount, the foundation from which the service is efficiently delivered is key. This means, institutions with exceedingly large infrastructure may need to divest some of their assets to keep expenses at more manageable levels. For some institutions, this would mean the elimination of programs that do not draw viable enrollment numbers. Management attributes such as planning, task execution, and the ability to motivate are essential attributes of institutions (Floud & Corner, 2007). Universities benefit from effective strategic management anchored on quality teaching and student-centered experiences, cultivating a research-oriented and enterprising culture, and accessing external financial resources to fund and incubate innovative academic ideas (Schram,

2011). Consulting firms such as Docere Group International, owned and operated by the editors, have started to help academic institutions transition into a business mindset and creatively find strategic partners and capital to grow.

Market sensitive. Academic institutions need to be aware of market conditions in the local, national, and international level. Institutions need to intensify their research efforts to keenly understand market influences and craft timely strategies to capture opportunities and address challenges. There is a growing need to carefully examine competitive activities and plan effective courses of action. If President Obama's January 2015 proposal for free tuition and unlimited access to the nation's community colleges is ultimately funded and enacted, the rest of higher education will have to adapt quickly—with implications for existing revenue streams and market approaches for many undergraduate institutions as well as the need to plan for a more robust and diverse population of students headed to the undergraduate upper division and beyond.

Organizationally fit. Organizational health is essential for academic institutions. Business models have to be decentralized to guarantee a fast response time to challenges and opportunities—which alone would represent a huge "sea change" for this notoriously ponderous sector. Academic bureaucracy and red tape have to be cut to ensure consistent operational efficiency. Universities need to be able to function in a lean, strong, and agile manner—again, a gigantic sea change from the "Ivory Tower's" storied insulation, isolation, and self-congratulatory norms and hallowed traditions for conducting its affairs. Governance models will have to change to reflect these new realities. Universities face countless risks, and enterprise risk management is essential with due consideration provided for internal environment, objectives setting, event identification, risk assessment, risk response, control activities, information and communication, and monitoring (Association of Governing Boards, 2007). Proper administrative control along with financial access helps reduce operational risk (European University Association, 2008). Effective measurement systems are important with the careful selection of performance indicators and reward systems (Abbey, 2007).

Student-centered. With intense competition, institutions who know their students well offer the best value, and who have mastered student recruitment gain the competitive advantage. A Gallup (2014) report indicated that long-term outcomes for college students were shaped by the support and relationships they built while in college. For instance, in scenarios where there were caring professors, teachers who stimulated excitement in learning, or individuals who encouraged the pursuit of their dreams, the college experience became more meaningful. Institutions will need to be in tune with student needs. They have to take proactive efforts in attracting and keeping students and ensuring their professional success. Already a generation ago, those of us who teach at the graduate level recognized an appalling lack of foundational preparation in our students and often had to incorporate remediation in areas such as critical thinking and the ability to write an academic paper into our course design. There is little indication that this problem has gone away, with significant implications for the work required in K-12 and undergraduate preparation.

Academic institutions need to closely link strategic policy formation with execution and provide keen attention to factors such as direction, communication, sponsorship, actions, accountability, resources, incentives, measurement, engagement, feedback, and passion and enthusiasm (Kennie, 2007).

In decades past, academic institutions have proven themselves to be resilient and innovative. Many have survived natural calamities, wars, financial crisis, and a host of other challenges. Many have decided to do the "right" thing and serve the best interests of stakeholders.

In the end, the strategic path taken by the university's leadership team sealed their fate and destiny. In a contemporary world where governments, markets, stakeholders, students, competition, and technologies continually evolve and redefine the operational terrain, the university's ability to pick the right strategy and execute it well at the right time is paramount.

References

Abbey, C. (2007). What can performance indicators do for higher education institutions? A US perspective. In B. Conraths & A. Trusso (Eds.) *Managing the University Community, Exploring Good Practice*. Accessed December 30, 2014. Available at: http://www.eua.be/fileadmin/user_upload/files/Publications/Managing_the_University_Community.pdf

Association of Governing Boards. (2007). Meeting the challenges of enterprise risk management in education. A joint research project with National Association of College and University Business Officers (NACUBO). Accessed January 1, 2015. Viewable at: http://www.ucop.edu/enterprise-risk-management/_files/agb_nacubo_hied.pdf

Cohen, S. (2014). A quick way to cut college costs. Accessed January 1, 2015. Viewable at: http://www.nytimes.com/2014/03/21/opinion/a-quick-way-to-cut-college-costs.html?_r=0

Economist. (2014). Making college cost less. Accessed January 1, 2015. Available at: http://www.economist.com/news/leaders/21600120-many-american-universities-offer-lousy-value-money-government-can-help-change

Ernst, & Young. (2015). Future challenges for universities. Accessed January 1, 2015. Available at: http://www.ey.com/AU/en/Industries/Government---Public-Sector/UOF_Future-challenges-for-universities

European University Association. (2008). *Financially Sustainable Universities. Toward Full Costing in European Universities*. Brussels: European University Association.

Floud, R., & Corner, F. (2007). Managing a merger: Making it work for a university. In B. Conraths & A. Trusso (Eds.) *Managing the University Community, Exploring Good Practice*. Accessed December 30, 2014. Available at: http://www.eua.be/fileadmin/user_upload/files/Publications/Managing_the_University_Community.pdf

Gallup. (2014). Gallup Purdue Index. Accessed December 30, 2014. Available at: http://products.gallup.com/168857/gallup-purdue-index-inaugural-national-report.aspx

Kennie, T. (2007). Management and higher education: Is it really that necessary? In B. Conraths & A. Trusso (Eds.) *Managing the University Community, Exploring Good Practice*. Accessed December 30,

2014. Available at: http://www.eua.be/fileadmin/user_upload/files /Publications/Managing_the_University_Community.pdf

Sanchez, C. (2014). How the cost of college went from affordable to sky high. Accessed January 1, 2015. Viewable at: http://www.npr.org /2014/03/18/290868013/how-the-cost-of-college-went-from-affordable-to-sky-high

Schram, A. (2011). Development challenges for universities in developing nations. Accessed January 1, 2015. Available at: http://www .academia.edu/673174/Development_Challenges_for_Universities_in_ Developing_Nations

Index

List of Contributing Authors

1. Don Betz is the president of the University of Central Oklahoma, a public regional institution serving the Oklahoma City metro area. During his 45-year career in higher education, he has served as the president of Northeastern State University (Oklahoma) and Chancellor of the University of Wisconsin River Falls as well as provost at two universities. He was awarded the Medal of Excellence in University Teaching in Oklahoma and has been inducted into the Oklahoma Higher Education Hall of Fame. He has founded leadership programs at four institutions and pursued his career interest in international studies through service at the United Nations, as a Fulbright Presidential Fellow and by sponsoring study abroad programs.

2. Gary Bonvillian has served as the president of Thomas University in Thomasville, Georgia, since 2006. He has held both faculty and administrative roles in four other institutions over the past 38 years. As a Professor of Management, he has researched, taught, and consulted in the subject areas of leadership, change of management, organizational development, and quality principles. He is published in all of these topics to include serving as lead author on the Liberal Arts College Adapting to Change: The Survival of Small Schools, presented by Garland Publishing in 1996. He has been an invited chapter author in three other books.

3. Lisbeth Claus, Ph.D., SPHR, GPHR, SHRM-SCP, is a professor of Global HR at the Atkinson Graduate School of Management of Willamette University in Oregon (United States). Dr. Claus has been published widely in academic and professional journals on subject matters related to global HR. Her research focuses on the implications for global organizations when their employees cross borders. She is considered the leading expert on employer duty of care and informs employers of their obligation to protect their business travellers, international assignees, and dependents. She is

editor-in-chief of the *Global HR Practitioner Handbook* series (Global Immersion Press). She served as interim Associate Dean at the Atkinson Graduate School of Management and Acting Dean at the Monterey Institute of International Studies. She also held managerial positions at Safeway Inc. and Maritz Inc.

4. Gary Dill has served as the president of University of the Southwest since 2002. His prior professional experience includes 11 years of service in senior academic administration; 2 years in state department of education planning; 3 years as a university faculty member; and 12 years as a pastor in two denominations. Dill's academic credentials include a doctor of philosophy (Ph.D.) in higher education administration and ethics from the University of Texas at Austin [TX] and 2 years of postdoctoral study in philosophy and theology at the University of Notre Dame in South Bend [IN]. His theological degrees include a doctor of ministry (D.Min.) from Southern Baptist Theological Seminary in Louisville [KY], and a master of divinity (M.Div.) from Princeton Theological Seminary [NJ]. Philosophy and religion were his undergraduate majors at Houston Baptist University [TX], where he earned his bachelor's degree (B.A.). He is an ordained Presbyterian minister.

5. Fernando Galván is a professor of English and the president of the University of Alcalá, Madrid (Spain), appointed for the period 2010–2018. He has extensive experience as a researcher in literature and as an expert in University teaching and research evaluation for quality agencies in Spain, France, and Italy. He is presently a member of the Executive Committee of the International Association of University Presidents (IAUP), and has chaired (2007–2013) the European Society for the Study of English (ESSE), a federation of 33 national associations of English Studies across Europe.

6. Dr. Geetha Garib has worked as an assistant professor in Management and Organization at Tilburg University (The Netherlands) and researcher at the University College of London (UK). Her main research topics are diversity and social identity in the management field. She has published papers in several peer-reviewed journals on these topics (e.g., *International Journal of Hospitality*

Management and *Identity: an International Journal of Theory and Research*). Recently, she wrote a chapter on International Diversity Management in the book *Transcultural Marketing for Incremental and Radical Innovation* (2014). She is also actively involved in management research and consulting.

7. Dennis H. Holtschneider, CM, is the president of DePaul University and a lecturer in the Harvard University Management Development Program. He has served on the boards of the National Association of Independent Colleges (NAICU) and The Association of Catholic Colleges and Universities (ACCU), and presently, on the American Council of Education (ACE). In 2014, when this article was written, he was on sabbatical leave as Visiting Scholar of Higher Education at Harvard University's Graduate School of Education.

8. Dr. Neal King is the Chairman of the Board of Directors and President Emeritus of the International Association of University Presidents (IAUP). Professor of Psychology and former President of Antioch University Los Angeles, he sits on the Board of Directors of the World University Consortium (WUC), the Advisory Board for the Association of Universities of Asia and the Pacific (AUAP) and as Vice Chair of the Board of Governors and Distinguished Fellow at New Westminster College. King represents IAUP on the Multistakeholder Advisory Council for the United Nations Economic & Social Council (ECOSOC). Co-Editor of this volume, King is also Co-CEO of Docere Group International, a management consulting firm specialized in university turnaround and mergers and acquisitions.

9. Noel F. McGinn is Professor Emeritus from the Harvard University Graduate School of Education and Fellow Emeritus of the Harvard Institute for International Development. He has worked as an advisor to ministries of education and universities in 25 countries and has published on educational planning, school effectiveness, decentralization, and policy implementation.

10. Dr. J. Mark Munoz is a Professor of Management and International Business and Interim Dean at the Tabor School of Business at Millikin University. He was a former Visiting Fellow at the Kennedy School of Government at Harvard University. He is a recipient of several awards,

including three Best Research Paper Awards, an International Book Award, a literary award, and the ACBSP Teaching Excellence Award among others. Aside from top-tier journal publications, he has authored/edited/co-edited 10 books, namely *Land of My Birth, Winning Across Borders, In Transition, A Salesman in Asia, Handbook of Business Plan Creation, International Social Entrepreneurship, Contemporary Microenterprises: Concepts and Cases, Handbook on the Geopolitics of Business Hispanic-Latino Entrepreneurship*, and *Business Plan Essentials*. He was recognized as a Distinguished Scholar by the Academy of Global Business Advancement. He handles management consulting projects worldwide specifically in the areas of strategic planning, business development, finance, and mergers and acquisitions.

11. Dr. Mac Powell is the seventh president of John F. Kennedy University and led the institution to historic financial success, the receipt of the federal Hispanic Serving Institution designation, and in the transition to becoming a serving-learning institution. He serves as a Commissioner for the American Council of Education's Commission on Educational Attainment and Commissioner on the Western Association of Schools and Colleges Senior Commission, and he previously served as Editor-in-Chief of the Journal of Performance Psychology and Chair of the Council of Applied Master's Programs in Psychology. A graduate of the WASC Assessment Leadership Academy, Dr. Powell's recent scholarship focuses on the role of accreditation in consumer protection, educational attainment, and the challenges of rising tuition costs for students.

12. Ernesto Schiefelbein is the president of the Universidad Autonoma de Chile. He has also served as Minister of Education for Chile, Director of the Latin American Office of UNESCO, and program officer for the World Bank. He is the author of books on educational planning, educational finance, and determinants of student achievement. He has been awarded the Comenius Medal for his service to education.

13. Ralph A. Wolff served as the president of the Senior College Commission of the Western Association of Schools and Colleges (WASC) for 17 years, and led that agency toward new approaches

of accreditation that are student and organizational learning centered. Recently he was appointed to the National Advisory Committee on Institutional Quality and Integrity (NACIQI) of the U.S. Department of Education. He currently serves as an international consultant on quality assurance, strategic visioning, and innovation.

14. Thimios Zaharopoulos serves as Provost at DEREE—The American College of Greece. Previously, he held various positions at Park University, including Vice President for Global and Lifelong Learning, Special Assistant to the President, Interim Provost, and dean of the College of Liberal Arts and Sciences. He has also held teaching positions at Washburn University and Pittsburg State University. He has published two books, *Mass Media in Greece: Power, Politics and Privatization* and *Sports and Media* (in Greek), and numerous book chapters and refereed journal articles in the area of international communication and media effects. He has been a member of the Editorial Review Board of the *Journal of Radio and Audio Media* and has served as an outside evaluator for the Open University of Cyprus and the Aristotelian University of Greece.

CPSIA information can be obtained
at www.ICGtesting.com
Printed in the USA
FSOW03n0555170516
20391FS